Good News and How to Share It

The Bible Reading Fellowship
BRF encourages regular, informed Bible reading as a
means of renewal in churches.
BRF publishes three series of regular Bible Reading Notes:
New Daylight, Guidelines and *First Light.*
BRF publishes a wide range of materials for individual and
group study. These include resources for Advent, Lent,
Confirmation and the Decade of Evangelism.
Write or call now for a full list of publications:

The Bible Reading Fellowship
Peter's Way
Sandy Lane West
Oxford
OX4 5HG
Tel: 0865 748227

Good News and How to Share It

MICHAEL GREEN

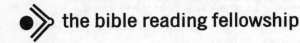 the bible reading fellowship

Text Copyright © Michael Green 1993

The author asserts the moral right
to be identified as the author of this work

Published by
The Bible Reading Fellowship
Peter's Way
Sandy Lane West
Oxford
OX4 5HG
ISBN 0 7459 2580 4

First edition 1993

Acknowledgments

Unless otherwise acknowledged, Scripture quotations are taken
from the Holy Bible, New International Version. Copyright © 1973,
1978, 1984 by International Bible Society. Used by permission of
Hodder and Stoughton Limited.

A catalogue record for this book is available
from the British Library

Printed and bound by Cox & Wyman Ltd, Reading

Contents

Dedicated to
Martin Cavender and Bishop Michael Marshall
my colleagues in 'Springboard',
an Initiative by the Archbishops of Canterbury and York
during the Decade of Evangelism.

A note from the Editor

I wonder why you have bought this book? I hope for at least two reasons.

You will be wanting to think more deeply about the Good News—the marvellous message of the Christian faith, about forgiveness, about new life, and about the immense and wonderful love of God.

You will also be wanting to think about how to share the Good News—and you will probably want to do this together with other people in your church.

So after each chapter in this book there is material for you to use in groups. Michael Green has provided the questions for discussion. And he has asked me to provide additional material, with meditations and prayers.

Some of you will be experts at running discussion and prayer groups, and therefore you will work out your own ways of handling them. But others of you may be beginners—so there is material here for you to use as you wish. Those of you who have run groups before will know the great benefit of starting with a very simple supper. Sharing a meal makes it far easier to share the things of God. It was in the sharing of a meal that Jesus gave to his disciples for all time the sacrament which shows us the self-giving love of God.

It is vital to pray in the subject we are studying, as well as looking at what it says and what it means. So there are prayers here for you to use if you wish. Some have been written for the Decade of Evangelism by churches all over the world, collected and circulated by The Anglican Consultative Council. Others have been taken from *The Lion Prayer Collection*, compiled by Mary Batchelor.

Silence is an important part of prayer. As we are silent in the presence of God he can speak to our heart—and say what he wants to say. In a silence God will speak to us as individuals as well as to our church—if only we will listen. So there are meditations here as well, with suggestions for times of silence.

Canon Michael Green is one of the two advisers (Bishop Michael Marshall is the other) to the Archbishops of Canterbury and York in their Springboard Initiative for the Decade of Evangelism. He is himself a gifted and brilliant evangelist—through both his speaking and his writing. Now, in this book, Michael Green helps us with our own evangelism.

He tells us what the Good News of the Christian faith is, spelling it out in a way that makes it easy to share. Then he shows us how to share it—with our friends and with our neighbours. And that, of course, is what Jesus Christ told us to do.

Shelagh Brown
Commissioning Editor

Canon Dr Michael Green

8

Part One

Six Bible Studies on the Christian Faith

Introduction

I have just moved into a new home in Nottingham, after six years in Canada.

Yesterday Ian, a local vicar, came to see me, as a welcome. In the course of conversation he told me of a holiday club he and his fellow clergy had been running. In his group of eleven young people only one could come up with even *one* of the Ten Commandments. Significantly, it was 'Thou shalt not steal.' All the others were totally ignorant of that basic foundation of ethics world-wide, the Ten Commandments, although they all had some notional attachment to the church. 84 per cent of young people in Britain nowadays have no link at all with any church.

My mind went back to my recent experience in Western Canada. There the ignorance of the Christian faith is even deeper, and secularization even more pronounced. 'Christmas' now has disappeared into 'The Winter Festival'. The birth of Jesus is unknown by multitudes. They know nothing of the coming of God into the world on the first Christmas morning. All they know is the coming of endless Santas to the shops. Indeed, the schools are forbidden to have plays, songs or decorations at Christmas time which reflect the birth of Jesus. There is more Christianity in the schools of Moscow than there is in Vancouver. Needless to say, Easter has turned into the Spring Break, and Easter Bunnies are everywhere, while the resurrection of Jesus is a well-kept secret.

'Hang on,' you may be thinking. 'We are not like that. This book comes from the Bible Reading Fellowship. Many of us read the Bible regularly. Many of us are faithful Anglican Christians, and have been for many years.' I fully take the point of that. However, tell me this. Is it not all too easy for us to have been regular churchgoers for a long time, yet to be hard put to it to have a clear understanding of what the Christian faith is really about? And don't we sometimes feel very ill-equipped if we are asked to explain the heart of the faith to someone who is interested in knowing more about it?

We live in a generation when Christianity is vibrant in Asia, Africa, and Latin America, but is very much under assault, explicit and implicit, in the West. This trend cannot be reversed by the clergy alone. Indeed the clergy cannot have a lot of influence in outreach anyway, because people will think, 'Well, they're paid to talk about God.' The uncommitted will only sit up and take notice when church members in general are clear and confident about their faith, and are keen, when opportunity offers, to share it with others. Christianity has been a missionary faith from the outset. It is not something private to keep to ourselves, and it never has been. We have good news. And it is our business to share it.

Mercifully, such sharing is not difficult, although we often think it is. We feel that someone will need to go to a theological college for several years before attempting it. No way! The first followers of Jesus were mainly semi-educated working men who had got thrilled with Jesus. And if you are thrilled, you won't find it hard to let it show! Now that intrigues people. They never imagined the Christian faith was something to get excited about!

Do I sense you cringing at that word 'excited'? Is this yet another book directed towards extrovert enthusiasts? Not at all. We all get excited in different ways, depending on our personality. But if we are persuaded of the tremendous worth of any project, it becomes abundantly plain in the zeal with which we pursue it—however different our ways of showing 'excitement' may be! That is one of the lovely things in God's plan. He has chosen a Church that is like a body. It is composed of different limbs and parts, and each one expresses the life which they all share in a different way. The leg is not called to act like an ear: simply to be itself—with the bloodstream coursing through. It's like that with Christ's 'Body', the Church. We are meant to be ourselves, and let the bloodstream of his life flow through us in the way that comes naturally for us.

This little book is intended to help that natural outflow. It is based on material from the Bible, the title deeds of the Christian religion. We shall in fact be looking into twelve Bible studies, and will be expecting a clear, uncomplicated answer to two questions. The first six studies are concerned with what is the heart of the Christian faith. And the second six are about how we can begin to share it with other people—in a natural, relaxed way.

So read on, and let's enjoy ourselves! We have such a lot to be thankful for.

We worship a God who has not left us to stumble around in the dark, but has revealed himself to us—in the Scriptures, in nature, and, supremely, in Jesus Christ.

We worship a God who wants us to use our minds as well as our hearts, and to understand something, at least, of what we believe.

We worship a God who loves all people. Like a lover with his beloved he longs for them to respond to his love. And God wants you and me to be part of the action. He wants us to tell them the good news of the enormous love which he has for them, and the forgiveness he

11

offers them. Then, when they have said 'Yes' to God, he wants them to join with us in his service. That is what the first followers of Jesus told the world after the resurrection, and the message is still the same.

That which was from the beginning, which we have heard, which we have seen with our eyes, which we have looked at and our hands have touched—this we proclaim concerning the Word of life. The life appeared; we have seen it and testify to it, and we proclaim to you the eternal life, which was with the Father and has appeared to us. We proclaim to you what we have seen and heard, so that you also may have fellowship with us. And our fellowship is with the Father and with his Son, Jesus Christ.

1 John 1:1–3

1 My God Is Real

For this is what the Lord says—he who created the heavens, he is God; he who fashioned and made the earth, he founded it; he did not create it to be empty, but formed it to be inhabited—he says: 'I am the Lord, and there is no other. I have not spoken in secret, from somewhere in a land of darkness; I have not said to Jacob's descendants, "Seek me in vain." I, the Lord, speak the truth; I declare what is right. Gather together and come; assemble, you fugitives from the nations. Ignorant are those who carry about idols of wood, who pray to gods that cannot save. Declare what is to be, present it—let them take counsel together. Who foretold this long ago, who declared it from the distant past? Was it not I, the Lord? And there is no God apart from me, a righteous God and a Saviour; there is none but me. Turn to me and be saved, all you ends of the earth; for I am God and there is no other. By myself I have sworn, my mouth has uttered in all integrity a word that will not be revoked: Before me every knee will bow; by me every tongue will swear. They will say of me, "In the Lord alone are righteousness and strength." ' All who have raged against him will come to him and be put to shame. But in the Lord all the descendants of Israel will be found righteous and will exult.

Isaiah 45:18–25

This passage takes us right to the heart of the Christian (and Jewish) understanding of God. We human beings cannot fully understand the mysterious source of our own existence and that of our cosmos. This passage recognizes that, and it is only one of many that could have been chosen. But because God has generously disclosed something of himself it is gloriously possible for us to get to know him, and to start to understand the mystery of his person. Here are seven things about him of which we may be quietly confident.

1. **God is real.** God is contrasted here to 'idols'—and his worshippers are contrasted to those who 'pray to gods who cannot save'. But how can we know he is real? We can't prove it scientifically, but there are many pointers to that truth. Here are some of them.

◆ First, the world we live in. What accounts for it? Why is there something rather than nothing? It just will not do to assign it all to chance. Not only is that intrinsically improbable in the highest degree, but if it was all due to chance, our world would not operate on the universal basis of cause and effect. If everything we do, everything we experience in this world has a cause, then so did the world itself. And that brings us directly to God.

◆ Secondly, design in the world. If the physical circumstances of our world had been even a tiny fraction different, there could have been no life on this earth. Scientists are talking these days about the 'anthropic principle'. By this they mean that the world shows every mark of having been constructed with us in mind. Think of the design in the complex apparatus of an eye, or ear, or embryo. It is highly unconvincing to say that it has no Designer.

◆ Thirdly, a fact which cannot be denied is human reason and creativity. It is difficult to give a convincing explanation for these on the assumption that we are 'naked apes' or 'grown up genes'. It is interesting to note that all atheist arguments rely heavily on *reason*, which, on their assumptions, has no independent validity at all. No, it is far more rational to believe that reason and creativity are precious gifts of the supremely creative Intelligence we call God.

◆ Fourthly, human personality. That's what makes us different from an animal, a dead body or a robot. There is great difficulty in supposing (as atheists *have* to suppose) that the personal springs from the impersonal, that we are nothing more than a collection of atoms. No, there is only one explanation of human personality which makes sense—that we come from a personal source. That source we call God.

◆ Fifthly, our values. These values we all cherish—truth, beauty, goodness, creativity, love. Where do they come from? On the materialist's assumptions they cannot come from a source beyond ourselves. Indeed, on a materialist's view there is no compelling reason why we should all value them. But if there is a Creator God, then our values make sense. They are planted within us by God, the supreme Value, and each of them sheds light on some aspect of his nature.

◆ Sixthly, conscience. We all have a conscience. We know intuitively that there is a difference between right and wrong. When conscience is at work we do not act because we hope to gain anything out of it, or because we fear the consequences if we refuse. Conscience says to us, 'This is right. Do it!' It is like a moral law within our hearts. And a law like that points to a Law-giver.

◆ Seventhly, religion. The fact of the matter is that, despite the prevalence of scepticism in some Western countries, no nation has ever existed (so far as we can tell) where the worship of some god or other has not been widespread. There is a deeply rooted instinct in human beings to worship. All our other instincts and desires have an appropriate fulfilment: hunger is met by food, exhaustion by sleep, our sexual instinct by intercourse, and so on. Is religion the only instinct we have where there is no reality for it to relate to?

15

Certainly the burden of proof is on the person who argues like that. It is much more natural to assume that the universal fact of religion is a firm pointer towards the reality of God.

We have spent some time looking at the reality of God, because these days that is often denied or discounted. But this chapter has several other important things to say about God which we cannot neglect if we are to get a rounded picture of him.

2. **God is the Only.** There is only one God. That is what this passage, like so many others in the Bible, is saying. Just one God, and no runners up! 'I am the Lord, and there is no other.' That is the claim, and it is impossible for Christians to surrender it.

The religious instinct of mankind has been grievously corrupted. Sometimes a religion maintains there are many gods: that was the case with Greek and Roman religion. Sometimes it worships and seeks to placate spirits, as in animism in many parts of our world. Sometimes the divine is seen as impersonal, as in Hinduism and Buddhism. Sometimes people are almost forced to worship a human being in the place of God: think of Stalin or Hitler.

But over against all these corruptions, Christians maintain that there is only one God, that he is personal, and that he is is far greater than we are. This transcendent, personal God shines out against the dark background of confusion and distortion which gathers round the whole notion of God these days—not least in the amalgam of beliefs which go to make up the 'New Age'. There is only one God. That is fundamental.

3. **God is the Creator.** God is described here (and everywhere in Scripture) as 'he who created the heavens . . . he who fashioned and made the earth, he founded it; and did not create it to be empty, but formed it to be inhabited.' To believe this does not commit us to 'creationism' over against evolution. But it does commit us to the conviction that behind whatever evolutionary processes there may have been, God almighty, the Only One, was actively at work. He has a purpose for this world. He did not create it to be empty but to be inhabited. Every person, every tree, every flower discloses his infinite variety and creative vision. In a world where life is so often cheap, and

16

the environment so carelessly destroyed, Christians are resolute in what they maintain: that God is no petty deity simply to be worshipped in a church on Sunday for an hour, after which we have done our duty and God has been satisfied. Rather, God is the sovereign, awesome Creator of the whole universe, from the furthest star in the furthest galaxy to you and me and all things and all creatures on our little planet earth. If that does not drive us to our knees in adoring worship, I don't know what will.

4. **God is the revealer.** That is very wonderful and very comforting. God wants us to know him. And so he has revealed himself to us. You will not find that in any of the religions of the world. Even Islam believes that Allah has not revealed *himself* to us but has only revealed his will. Not so with the God of the Old and New Testaments. 'I have not spoken in secret, from somewhere in a land of darkness.' No, he reveals himself to us so that we may know him and respond to him. If it were not so, God would be in inaccessible, would he not? How could we who are very finite and very sinful possibly get through to the Absolute and the Holy? It could not be done. And God knew it.

So he did not leave us to blunder on in the darkness, comparing our different ideas of what God was like. He revealed himself. And he did it in several ways.

◆ Partly through human personality: as we have seen, he created us, in some sense, 'in his own image'.

◆ Partly through the course of history, particularly the history of his saving acts for his people Israel, through whom he planned to make himself known to the world.

◆ Partly through the Scriptures.

◆ Finally through his personal intervention onto the stage of human history in the person of Jesus.

He is the God who does not hide himself: he discloses himself. He wants us to know him.

5. **God is the Holy One.** The word 'holy' is not used here, but the idea certainly is, and the concept is prevalent throughout the Bible. God is absolutely upright and just and fair. He is not only moral and just in himself: he is also the very *source* of morality and justice. 'I, the Lord, speak the truth. I declare what is right.' And that is the ultimate safeguard against the corruption of the notion of God. It is also the ultimate challenge to our own speech and behaviour.

There is no real equivalent for the word 'holy'. It stands by itself. But we have an instinctive recognition of what it is when we see someone who has this character—think of Mother Teresa, or of Billy Graham. Both bring with them an intense sense of the presence of God when you meet them.

In the wonderful imagery of the apostle Paul, we are told that God 'lives in unapproachable light' (1 Timothy 6:16). That gives us some idea of what 'holy' means. But if we can't even approach the light that he dwells in, then doesn't that inevitably rule us out of any possibility of having a relationship with him? Mercifully no. 'For this is what the high and lofty One says—he who lives for ever, whose name is holy: "I live in a high and holy place, but also with him who is contrite and lowly in spirit" ' (Isaiah 57:15). But how can this be?

6. **God is the Saviour.** 'There is no God apart from me, a righteous God and a Saviour; there is none but me. Turn to me and be saved, all you ends of the earth; for I am God, and there is no other.' We can only have a relationship with a God who is so utterly above us, so utterly holy, if he finds some way of rescuing us from our self-centredness and our failures. Let's be blunt—from our sins.

We have offended this holy God. There is no way we can earn our forgiveness, because a good deed doesn't wipe out a bad one. If I am taken to court and found guilty of fraud, the judge will be unimpressed and unmoved if I tell him that I drive impeccably and have never once driven over the speed limit. We have, in the words of the Prayer Book, 'offended against thy holy laws', and we have to pay the penalty. But the penalty is spiritual death, so we are in a terrible predicament. Trying hard and going to church won't get us out of it—though many people think it will. What we need is to be rescued. And if there is to be rescue, God must provide it: I know that you and I cannot. And the marvellous thing is that from one end of Scripture to the other God

18

reveals himself as the Saviour, the Rescuer. This is a tremendous comfort to the people who are humble enough to 'turn to him and be saved'—but it is profoundly humiliating to the self-satisfied.

Christianity is unashamedly a rescue religion: that is why so many respectable people fight shy of it! Just how God could be both 'righteous' and 'Saviour' we shall examine in our next two studies. Enough for the moment that he is.

7. **God is judge.** We can't leave that out. He is the moral ruler of the universe. Evil must be dealt with—if not at once, then later. And it will. 'Before me every knee will bow,' God says in our passage—and one day that will happen. 'In the Lord alone are righteousness and strength. All who have raged against him will come to him and be put to shame.' There will be no conscripts in heaven. Those who refuse his way of rescue will only have themselves to blame. It sounds tough, but it is fair. It would be terrible if evil did not in the end get punished. Terrible if God—a holy God—pretended that good and evil were ultimately a matter of indifference to him. God's 'strange work' of judgment is the other side of the coin from his mercy. They belong together. Together they form two poles of the divine nature, and the Bible always holds the two together.

What a marvellous passage we have been looking at, bringing together as it does no less than seven central aspects of the God we worship. This is our God. And he is real!

Group material, meditation and prayers

A prayer for the Decade of Evangelism from the Church in West Malaysia:

Almighty God, we thank you for having renewed your Church, at various times and in various ways, by rekindling the fire of love for you through the work of your Holy Spirit. Rekindle your love in our hearts and renew us to fulfil the Great Commission which your Son committed to us; so that, individually and collectively, as members of your Church, we may help many to know Jesus

Christ as their Lord and Saviour. Empower us by your Spirit to
share, with our neighbours and friends, our human stories in the
context of your divine story; through Jesus Christ our Lord. Amen.

Have a brief silence after that prayer (not less than one minute, not more than two). If you are not used to silences, time it. Then read out Isaiah 45:18–25 slowly. It is the passage at the start of the chapter.

Ask every person in the group to say briefly, in one or two sentences, why they have come and what they hope might result from it.

Then discuss the following questions.

1. What to you is the most convincing evidence for the reality of God?

2. If God is the Creator, how should it affect our attitude both to the environment and to our daily work?

3. Does the notion of God as Rescuer and Judge have any place in the teaching of your local church. If not, why might that be?

4. Can you talk meaningfully about 'being saved' these days?

Meditation

As you read this out, let there be peaceful spaces in between the phrases.

Will you all close your eyes. Be still, and be comfortable. It's best to sit up, with your back straight, not rigid, but relaxed. Have your feet flat on the floor, and your hands on your knees. Be aware of the chair you are sitting on, supporting you, holding you up. Be aware of your own breathing. Be aware of other people around you, and their breathing. Now listen to the word of God in the prophet Isaiah. (Read out slowly, with pauses between each phrase.)

To whom, then, will you compare God? What image will you compare him to? . . . Do you not know? Have you not heard? Has it not been told you from the beginning? Have you not understood since the earth was founded? He sits enthroned above the circle of the earth, and its people are like grasshoppers. He stretches out the heavens like a canopy, and spreads them out like a tent to live in ... 'To whom will you compare me? Or who is my equal?' says the Holy One. Lift your eyes and look to the heavens. Who created all these? He who brings out the starry host one by one, and calls them each by name. Because of his great and mighty strength, not one of them is missing. Why do you say, O Jacob, and complain, O Israel, 'My way is hidden from the Lord; my cause is disregarded by my God'? Do you not know? Have you not heard? The Lord is the everlasting God, the Creator of the ends of the earth. He will not grow tired or weary, and his understanding no-one can fathom. He gives strength to the weary and increases the power of the weak. Even youths grow tired and weary, and young men stumble and fall; but those who hope in the Lord will renew their strength. They will soar on wings like eagles; they will run and not grow weary, they will walk and not be faint.

Isaiah 40:18, 21–22, 25–31

Be silent for one or two minutes, and then say 'Our God is real ... Lord God, we worship you ...' After that, ask people to pray their own prayers aloud, if they wish to.

Final prayers

A prayer for the Decade of Evangelism from the Church in Japan:

Eternal and ever-loving Creator God, you who desire not the death of sinners, but rather delight that they may return to live with you, we ask you to look lovingly upon all your people, and especially to give to those who have had no chance to know you the heart to pay reverence to you, and increase the faith, the hope, and the love within them. Send your Holy Spirit to your Church at this Decade of Evangelism, especially on us who pray and serve your call, that we may be used as the instruments of your peace, the witnesses and the proclaimers to share the good news of your Son Jesus Christ. And, with all whom you love, give us the joy to

21

enter into your eternal Kingdom, through the blessings of the Saviour, Jesus Christ our Lord. Amen.

Now unto the King eternal, immortal, invisible, the only wise God, be honour and glory for ever and ever. Amen.

Heavenly Father, you have promised through your Son Jesus Christ that when we meet in his name, and pray according to his mind, he will be among us and will hear our prayer. In your love and wisdom fulfil our desires, and give us your greatest gift, which is to know you, the only true God, and Jesus Christ our Lord, who is alive and reigns with you and the Holy Spirit, one God, now and for ever. Amen.

Alternative Service Book

---

2   The Man Who is God

In the beginning was the Word, and the Word was with God, and the Word was God. He was with God in the beginning. Through him all things were made; without him nothing was made that has been made. In him was life, and that life was the light of men. The light shines in the darkness, but the darkness has not understood it. There came a man who was sent by God; his name was John. He came as a witness to testify concerning that light, so that through him all men might believe. He himself was not the light; he came only as a witness to the light. The true light that gives light to every man was coming into the world. He was in the world, and though the world was made through him, the world did not recognise him. He came to that which was his own, but his own did not receive him. Yet to all who received him, to those who believed in his name, he gave the right to become children of God—children born not of natural descent, nor of human decision or a husband's will, but born of God. The Word became flesh, and made his dwelling among us. We have seen his glory, glory of the One and Only, who came from the Father, full of grace and truth.

John 1:1–14

No one has ever seen God, but God the One and Only, who is at the Father's side, made him known.

John 1:18

There is something very remarkable about Christianity. No other faith is dependent upon the person of its founder. Islam, for example, is rightly proud of the life and godliness of Mohammed. Confucianism is rightly full of admiration for Confucius. But the teachings of Mohammed and of Confucius would stand whether or not their authors had ever lived. It is the teachings of these men, not their persons, that are important. Not so with Christianity. That depends not so much on the teachings of Jesus as on his person. Take away the person of Jesus from Christianity and nothing significant remains.

What, then, is so special about Jesus? It is widely accepted that he lived and taught wonderful things. The evidence for his miracles is extremely powerful. He is unquestionably one of the most influential men who ever lived. Most people would be happy to acclaim him as the greatest of teachers. But that can never satisfy the Christian. We are unwilling to put Jesus on the same shelf as Mohammed, Confucius, Buddha and the others in the supermarket of religions. 'I know men,' said Napoleon. 'And Jesus Christ was no mere man.'

What *was* so special about Jesus? Born of humble parents in a province on the edge of the Roman map, executed in shame on a public gallows some thirty years later—what makes him so special?

The first Christians had a very clear answer to this question, and none put it more sharply than John the Evangelist. But though I choose this passage because it is read so often in church and is so well known, it would be a mistake to that think its teaching is unique. It is not. Its teaching was common coin among the first Christians, and it might be helpful to glance at two other New Testament writers, to allow its force to strike us afresh. Listen to what Paul says about Jesus:

He is the image of the invisible God, the firstborn over all creation. For by him all things were created: things in heaven

24

and on earth, visible and invisible, whether thrones or powers or rulers or authorities; all things were created by him and for him. He is before all things, and in him all things hold together. And he is the head of the body, the church; he is the beginning and the firstborn from among the dead, so that in everything he might have the supremacy. For God was pleased to have all his fulness dwell in him.

Colossians 1:15–19

The Colossians were believers in Jesus, to be sure. But it was Jesus among all the other contenders of the day—'thrones', 'powers', 'rulers' and the like. Paul maintains some devastating differences.

◆ Jesus was the Creator: he shared this function with his heavenly Father.

◆ Jesus has the priority over all spiritual forces: they are simply not in the same league.

◆ Jesus is the origin and the goal of the whole universe.

◆ Jesus is the principle of coherence that holds all things together, including the laws of nature on which we depend.

◆ Jesus is the one who has broken the power of death.

◆ This Jesus is the head of the body, the Church.

◆ The whole fullness of God resides in Jesus.

Could you possibly make any stronger case for the complete supremacy of Jesus? He is the cosmic Christ. He is the Number One in the whole universe.

The other passage which leaves us in no doubt as to who Jesus is comes in the first verses of the Epistle to Hebrew Christians. We do not know the author, but he clearly came from the inner circle of the first Christians. This is what he had to say:

In the past God spoke to our forefathers through the prophets at many times and in various ways, but in these last days he has spoken to us by his Son, whom he appointed heir of all things, and through whom he made the universe. The Son is the radiance of God's glory, and the exact representation of his being, sustaining all things by his powerful word. After he had provided purification for sins, he sat down at the right hand of the Majesty in heaven.

Hebrews 1:1–4

Those words wash over us sonorously and soporifically as the Epistle at Christmas Communion. But think of what they are saying.

They maintain that Jesus is the fulfilment of God's self-disclosure. He is God's last word to humanity. There is nothing more to say. What more exhaustive and ultimate revelation could God give to us about himself than to come in person among us?

They tell us that this climactic revelation came not in a book but in a life, the life of God's only Son. And in case we may be in any doubt about who this Jesus is, the writer spells it out in detail. He is both the author and the goal of the universe. He made it, in cooperation with his heavenly Father, and it was all created for him: he is the 'heir'. Moreover, Jesus corresponds as closely to his heavenly Father as a sunbeam to the sun, or the stamp in the wax to the die which makes it. He is the principle by which the whole cosmos hangs together. He lies behind the laws of nature, sustaining all things by his power.

This cosmic Christ is the Church's Christ. He made purification for sins once for all upon the cross. And he is now in the place of power in the universe, seated at the right hand of his heavenly Father.

How different this majestic understanding of Jesus is from that of many a church member, who sees Jesus, perhaps, as one of the ways to God—but not *the* way; as a great religious leader—but not the physical expression, in space and time, of the eternal God Almighty.

And that is precisely what John is seeking to express in the famous passage with which we began and to which we now turn. He has no doubt who Jesus is. And he expresses it in terms which would have been familiar to his readers in the first century. 'The Word' was used as much in common language then as 'quantum' is today. It was the term used for the ultimate colleague of God in creation: the Jews used it of the divine 'wisdom'. And John wasn't only writing to Jews. He was writing to Greeks as well. For them the logos, or the word, was the rational power of God which created the whole universe and kept everything going.

John takes this well-known concept of the Word and boldly identifies it with Jesus. And how appropriate it is! Just as I cannot know what is in your mind unless you clothe it in 'word', so we cannot know what is in the mind of God unless he does the same. John proclaims that this is precisely what God has done. Jesus reveals the God we cannot see as closely as your words reveal the thoughts I could not grasp. 'The Word became flesh'—God's Word. That is who Jesus is.

Look at what John claims for the Word. He maintains first and foremost that the Word is God. Not a great teacher, not a wonder worker, but God, no less. And in the verses that follow he fills out that claim.

The Word was the agent in creation. He shared with the Father in the creation of the world. St John is as certain as St Paul and the writer of Hebrews that Jesus is no great guru, but God incarnate.

The Word is, moreover, 'the life'. The life-giving principle throughout nature, and supremely in human beings, is an aspect of Jesus. All life derives from him.

The Word is 'the light of men', and Jesus said, 'I am the light of the world.' The person of Jesus attracts men and women the world over who are open to goodness. He is the light. His teaching is light. His lifestyle is light. His death and resurrection are a veritable beacon. Jesus is 'the light of men' and to reject him is to walk in darkness. That is not to deny that there are many candles in this dark world. Socrates was a candle. Gandhi was a candle. But Jesus is no candle. He is the sun, shining in its strength.

Does this seem an exaggeration? John is aware of that objection, too, and so he says, 'The light shines in darkness but the darkness has not understood it.' There's a sturdy realism here: John knows that 'darkness' is a frank description of our society. And the darkness has never understood Jesus of Nazareth, the Light of the world. Actually a more probable translation of the Greek would be 'the darkness has never extinguished' the Light. And manifestly, that is the case.

The next verses in this amazing passage make Jesus the centre of our witness. It is Jesus whom we ought to be presenting, and talking about, just as John the Baptist did. If church members were willing to tell friends the difference Jesus has made to their lives, there is no telling what impact that would have.

But Jesus, the life of mankind, the light of the world, is no bland figure to whom all are polite. He has always attracted a lot of opposition from the forces of darkness. 'The world did not recognise him'—and that is still the case. He came to the world he had made, and his very own people did not want to know. There is something in human beings that is intrinsically opposed to the goodness and the ultimate claims that reside in Jesus of Nazareth.

Nevertheless the shocking truth stands firm. It is he, and he alone, who can gain entrance for us into the Royal Family, the family of God. It is, John tells us, only those who 'receive' Jesus and 'believe in' him who are welcomed by his heavenly Father. It is not a matter of trying hard. It is not a matter of going to church. It is a matter of recognizing who Jesus is, and surrendering our lives to him. For he alone is the divine adoption agency. He is the way into the family of God.

And when we do respond to him in adoring love, as St John and his friends had done, we discover glory, 'the glory of the One and Only . . . full of grace and truth'. We see in Jesus the perfect reflection of the unutterable beauty of God. For that what he is. 'No-one has ever seen God,' John reminds us, 'but God the One and Only, who is at the Father's side, has made him known.'

That is what makes Jesus so special. That is what sets him apart from all the great religious teachers down the ages. He makes God known, without distortion: he embodies God.

And yet that is a dangerous half truth. If he were simply God, he could not truly be one of us, could not fully understand us. But John is quick to guard against that misconception. 'The Word became flesh,' he tells us. 'The Word', the highest concept in Judaism, chose to become flesh—one of us. He was really God, and really man. That is the mystery of the person of Jesus. We must never lose grasp of either terminal: through them flows the electricity of authentic Christianity. Almost all heresies begin with some misinterpretation of the person of Jesus. We shall never plumb the mystery of what it means to be both God and man; but if we hold firm to both assertions we shall not go far astray on the central truth of Christianity, the incarnation.

Group material, meditation and prayers

A Prayer for the Decade of Evangelism from the Church of Ghana, West Africa:

O God, You sent Your Son into the world to be its true light. Pour out upon the Church Your Holy Spirit. Use us to sow the seeds of truth in the minds of the people, moving them to faith, and bringing conviction of sin and the realization of who Jesus is. We pray that both pastors and laity will surrender their abilities, time, energy and goods to the cause of the Decade of Evangelism. Help us not to betray the universal dimensions of Your plan for idle dreams—but to show to your world the realities of the life, passion and resurrection of our Lord Jesus, by which He glorified You on earth, through Him who lives and reigns with You in the Unity of the Holy Spirit for ever. Amen.

After a brief silence of one or two minutes ask every person in the group to say briefly, in one or two sentences, what impact last week's meeting had on them. Then read out John 1:1–14, 18, which is the passage at the start of the chapter. Discuss the following questions:

1. Does it really matter what we think about the person of Jesus? Surely it is his teaching which is the important thing?

2. Some Christians have thought of Jesus as so divine as not really to be human at all. Some have seen him as so human that he is not divine at all. Why are both these simplifications disastrous?

3. If the incarnation really is true, what does that say about human value and destiny?

Meditation

As you read this out, let there be quiet spaces in between each phrase. Please keep your eyes open. Will you settle yourself comfortably in your chair, with your feet flat on the floor, with your hands on your knees, and be still. Now will you shut your eyes, and be aware of the darkness. Think of the darkness in our world. 'The people that sat in darkness have seen a great light ... they who sit in the valley of the shadow of death, on them has the light shined ...' As you keep your eyes closed, go on being aware of the darkness. And now, for a few moments, be aware of the silence. (Possibly allow this silence to continue for two or three minutes.) If God never spoke to us, how would we ever know him? But he has spoken. Listen now to the Word of God, spoken through the prophet Isaiah, about the Servant of the Lord:

And now the Lord says—he who formed me in the womb to be his servant to bring Jacob back to him and gather Israel to himself, for I am honoured in the eyes of the Lord, and my God has been my strength—he says: 'It is too small a thing for you to be my servant to restore the tribes of Jacob and bring back those of Israel I have kept. I will also make you a light for the Gentiles, that you may bring my salvation to the ends of the earth.'

Isaiah 49:5–6

Now let the words of Jesus sink into your heart:

I am the light of the world, he who follows me shall not walk in darkness, but shall have the light of life.

John 8:12

Now let the words of the Gospel of John sink into your heart:

In the beginning was the Word, and the Word was with God, and the Word was God ... The Word became flesh and made his dwelling among us. We have seen his glory, the glory of the One and Only, who came from the Father, full of grace and truth.

John 1:1, 14

Now listen to what the writer to the Hebrews said about Jesus:

In the past God spoke to our forefathers through the prophets at many times and in various ways, but in these last days he has spoken to us by his Son, whom he appointed heir of all things, and through whom he made the universe. The Son is the radiance of God's glory and the exact representation of his being, sustaining all things by his powerful word.

Hebrews 1:1–3

Final prayers

Meekness and majesty,
Manhood and Deity,
In perfect harmony,
The Man who is God.
Lord of eternity
Dwells in humanity,
Kneels in humility
And washes our feet.

O what a mystery,
Meekness and majesty.
Bow down and worship
For this is your God,
This is your God.

Graham Kendrick. Copyright © Make Way Music/Thankyou Music, 1986

A prayer for the Decade of Evangelism from the Diocese of West Malaysia:

O God, we thank you for redeeming the whole of humanity through the holy incarnation, the vicarious death, the victorious resurrection and the glorious ascension of our Lord and Saviour Jesus Christ; and for the great Commission given to us to proclaim the Gospel of Salvation throughout the whole world. Guide and strengthen us by Your Holy Spirit to proclaim the Gospel of your saving love to all nations, more especially in our own nation, with greater intensity—through our word and deed, during the Decade of Evangelism, through Jesus Christ our Lord. Amen.

3   God to the Rescue

Open your Bible in the middle and you will find yourself somewhere very near to one the most famous chapters in all Scripture, Isaiah 53. Isaiah is portraying the fate of the supreme Servant of the Lord.

He was despised and rejected by men, a man of sorrows, and familiar with suffering. Like one from whom men hide their faces he was despised, and we esteemed him not. Surely he took up our infirmities and carried our sorrows, yet we considered him stricken by God, smitten by him, and afflicted. But he was pierced for our transgressions, he was crushed for our iniquities; the punishment that brought us peace was upon him, and by his wounds we are healed. We all, like sheep, have gone astray, each of us has turned to his own way, and the Lord has laid on him the iniquity of us all. He was oppressed and afflicted, yet he did not open his mouth; he was led like a lamb to the slaughter, and as a sheep before her shearers is silent, so he did not open his mouth. By oppression and judgment he was taken away. And who can speak of descendants? For he was cut off from the land of the living; for the transgression of my people he was stricken. He was assigned a grave with the wicked, and with the rich in his death, though he had done no violence, nor was any deceit in his mouth.

Yet it was the Lord's will to crush him and cause him to suffer, and though the Lord makes his life a guilt offering, he will see his offspring and prolong his days, and the will of the Lord will prosper in his hand. After the suffering of his soul, he will see the light of life and be satisfied; by his knowledge my righteous servant will justify many, and he will bear their iniquities. Therefore I will give him a portion among the great, and he will divide the spoils with the strong, because he poured out his life unto death, and was numbered with the transgressors. For he bore the sin of many, and made intercession for the transgressors.

Isaiah 53:3–12

I have a feeling that it is no accident that this chapter should come in the very centre of the Bible. For its message is central to the whole book. It is the great theme of almost all the different writers who make up Holy Scripture. There is an awesome majesty about these words. They take us out of our depth. They speak of innocent suffering; worse still, of the innocent taking responsibility, in terrible anguish, for the evils committed by others.

Curiously enough this passage was virtually ignored down the centuries between its composition in Isaiah's day and the time of Jesus. Nobody was keen to fulfil a prophecy like that! And of course it did not fit anybody. No, it pointed forward to a day of which Isaiah probably had no conception, when the supreme Servant of the Lord would be hanging on that terrible cross in the darkness of God-forsakenness on Good Friday.

In this great chapter there is more than a hint of the light of Easter Day breaking through. Certainly the early Christians saw it as an amazing foreshadowing of the destiny of Jesus. Think of the Ethiopian treasurer in the Book of Acts, sitting in his chariot and reading this very passage. Philip the evangelist hears him reading out loud (as they did in those days) and offers help. 'Tell me, please,' asked the Ethiopian, 'who is the prophet talking about, himself or someone else?' Then Philip began with that very passage of Scripture and told him the good news about Jesus.

Or listen to Peter, reflecting on the death of Jesus: he makes no less than six allusions to Isaiah's prophecy.

Christ suffered for you, leaving you an example that you should follow his steps. 'He committed no sin and no deceit was found in his mouth.' When they hurled their insults at him, he did not retaliate; when he suffered, he made no threats. Instead, he entrusted himself to him who judges justly. He himself bore our sins in his body on the tree, so that we might die to sins and live for righteousness; by his wounds you have been healed. For you were like sheep going astray, but now you have returned to the Shepherd and Overseer of your souls.

1 Peter 2:21–25

And so it continued in subsequent centuries. Christians were clear that the prophecy of Isaiah had been fulfilled beyond all expectation in the death and resurrection of Jesus. The Bible begins by telling us of God coming to the rescue of our first parents when they had broken his laws and flouted his will. He had to judge them and reject them from the garden. Sin must be punished. But in his love he simply had to come to their rescue, and we find him, as the story puts it, making skins to cover them in their nakedness. At the end of the Bible we find the same emphasis on God the rescuer. Heaven resounds with praise to the God who has made it possible for us to be forgiven: 'You are worthy ... because you were slain, and with your blood you purchased men for God from every tribe and language and people and nation' (Revelation 5:9).

This is our God: he loves, he cares, he rescues. And right in the centre of the Bible we find this profoundly moving portrait of what God's rescue means, and what it cost.

The predictions are phenomenal. 'He was despised and rejected ...

he was oppressed and afflicted, yet he did not open his mouth ... By oppression and judgment he was taken away ... Who can speak of his descendants? He was assigned a grave with the wicked'—think of the thieves with whom he was executed—'and with the rich in death'— think of rich Joseph of Arimathea's tomb in which he was buried. And all this 'though he had done no violence, nor was any deceit in his mouth ... He poured out his life unto death and was numbered with the transgressors.' He even 'made intercession for the transgressors'—think of his prayer for his executioners.

It all fits like a glove, but we still have not come to the heart of the matter. There are four aspects of his rescue which we need to be clear about.

First, there is our sin. Sheer human wickedness. And it is a disease we all have. 'All we, like sheep, have gone astray, each of us has turned to his own way.' That is where the problem lies. All human beings, without exception, have declined to follow the Shepherd. Like sheep, we have all opted to go our own way. We may not have done anything we consider very bad. But we have gone our own way. We are rebels. What is more, we are all guilty of two words which come again and again in this passage, 'iniquity' and 'transgression.' Iniquity means that we have not been straight and honest and true. Transgression means that we have often known what God's will is, and have deliberately done the opposite. And all of this alienates us from God, and makes us subject to his punishment.

Secondly, there is his suffering. The suffering of Jesus took many shapes. He was 'familiar with suffering'. The suffering of being 'despised and rejected' by the very people he came to help. The suffering of our 'sorrows' and 'infirmities' with which he utterly identified. The suffering of an unjust trial and terrible oppression. The suffering of keeping silent like 'a sheep before her shearers'. The suffering of being 'pierced' by those cruel nails of the 'wounds' which gaped in hands and feet and side. But even this does not take us to the heart of his sufferings. Many other people have endured just as great physical and even mental sufferings as Jesus. The special, the unique thing about his suffering is brought before us with startling clarity and frequent repetition.

'He was pierced for our transgressions.' 'The punishment which brought us peace was upon him.' 'The Lord has laid on him the iniquity of us all.' 'For the transgression of my people was he stricken.' 'It was the Lord's will to crush him' (rather than us). 'The Lord makes his life a guilt offering.' In a word, 'he bore the sin of many'. Expressed in these many ways, the prophet is looking forward to what this silent sufferer would do: he would personally underwrite the bad debts of the whole world to the God we have offended. He would personally bear the responsibility, the guilt, of us all.

Do you say 'I don't understand it?' Neither do I. But I believe it with all my heart, and I thank God for it every day. He has shown himself to be absolutely holy and makes no compromises with evil. But he has also shown himself to be unquenchable love: he has himself borne the penalty which we incurred. But it cost him hell to win us back to heaven. How he loves!

Thirdly, I see hints, at least, of his resurrection. 'After the suffering of his soul he will see the light of life and be satisfied.' 'He will see his offspring and prolong his days.' The cross was not the end of Jesus of Nazareth. At the heart of our faith lies an empty cross and an empty tomb. He rose again on the first Easter day! Even death, the last and greatest enemy, could not hold him down. He is alive for ever. He can be encountered by each of us. Christians are the Community of the Resurrection. They are the people who have met the risen Jesus and have started to share their lives with him as an ever present Friend and Guide and Master.

Finally I see something of his achievement. This mighty death and resurrection of Jesus has tremendous results. He took our infirmities. He bought our peace. He healed our wounds. He bore the sins of many—as many as would turn to him and say 'Thank you.' By making his life a guilt offering, he has indeed prolonged his days and seen countless 'offspring', in 'bringing many sons to glory' (Hebrews 2:10). After his suffering he has indeed 'seen the light of life' afresh. God has highly exalted him, and 'given him a portion among the great'. For through his death on that cross in our place, the innocent in the place of the guilty, he has justified many, by bearing their iniquities.

To justify means to acquit. That is the standing of every Christian in the sight of God: not just forgiven, but acquitted. Their sins are like a horrible filthy burden and have been transferred to the broad shoulders of the Saviour. They are gone! And the law of a holy God, which can only bring foreboding to my heart, has no further claim against me. Its demands have been met—by another. No wonder Jesus can reflect on this whole rescue operation which cost him so dear, and pronounce himself 'satisfied'. No wonder the Christian finds himself caught up with the hymn writer, crying out:

> Ransomed, healed, restored, forgiven,
> Who like me his praise should sing?
> Praise him, praise him. Praise him, praise him,
> Praise the everlasting King.

Group material, meditation and prayers

A prayer for the Decade of Evangelism from the Church in Southern Africa:

> Lord Jesus Christ, in your great love for the world, you came to die that we may live and called us to follow you, to carry the gospel to the lost, and to extend your Kingdom of righteousness in this world of pain and suffering and fear. Give to us and your whole Church grace to hear your call and to obey your word; and set our hearts on fire with love for you and all humankind so that we may engage in bold and adventurous evangelism to turn many from darkness to light; and grant that, attempting great things for you, we may expect great things from you; who, with the Father and the Holy Spirit, are one God, now and for ever. Amen.

Follow the prayer with a moment or two or silence. Then ask people to turn in their Bibles to Isaiah chapter 53, and, as someone reads it aloud (from verse 3), to imagine the Ethiopian in the book of Acts sitting in his chariot under the Mediterranean sun and doing the same . . .

Now discuss the following questions.

1. Why can't we rescue ourselves? Why do we need God to do it?

2. 'Forgiveness is a beggar's refuge,' said George Bernard Shaw. 'We must pay our debts.' Was he right?

37

3. How can the cross and resurrection so long ago make any difference to us now?

4. Would it have mattered if there had been no resurrection?

Meditation

As you read this out, leave spaces in between the phrases.

Will you sit comfortably, with your eyes shut, with your back straight, but relaxed and not rigid. Let your feet rest flat on the floor. Perhaps let your hands rest on your knees, with the palms up, as a symbol of openness, of wanting to receive from God whatever he wants to give to you. Now, in your mind's eye, see a cross. There's a man nailed to the cross ... the Son of Man, the Son of God ... Jesus, in agony, and in love—love for us.

> For God so loved the world that he gave his one and only Son, that whoever believes in him shall not perish, but have eternal life. For God did not send his Son into the world to condemn the world, but to save the world through him.
>
> John 3:16–17

> In Christ God was reconciling the world to himself, not counting their trespasses against them, and entrusting to us the message of reconciliation. So we are ambassadors for Christ, God making his appeal thorugh us. We beseech you on behalf of Christ, be reconciled to God. For our sake he made him to be sin who knew no sin, so that in him we might become the righteousness of God.
>
> 2 Corinthians 5:19–21 (RSV)

Let those wonderful truths sink deep down into your heart. Do you know the truth of them? Will you be an ambassador for Christ? Will you tell the good news about him to a sad and needy world? Good news about forgiveness. Good news about a new life. A new life in this world and in the next.

If only for this life we have hope in Christ, we are to be pitied more than all men. But Christ has indeed been raised from the dead, the firstfruits of those who have fallen asleep. For since death came through a man, the resurrection of the dead comes also through a man. For as in Adam all die, so in Christ all will be made alive.

1 Corinthians 15:19–22

After a brief silence, ask people to pray their own prayers if they so wish.

Final prayers

Led like a lamb to the slaughter
In silence and shame,
There on Your back You carried a world
Of violence and pain.
Bleeding, dying, bleeding, dying.

You're alive, You're alive
You have risen, Alleluia!
And the power and the glory are given,
Alleluia Jesus to You.

Graham Kendrick. Copyright © Thankyou Music, 1983

Lord of all life and power,
who through the mighty resurrection of your Son
overcame the old order of sin and death
to make all things new in him:
grant that we, being dead to sin
and alive to you in Jesus Christ,
may reign with him in glory;
to whom with you and the Holy Spirit
be praise and honour, glory and might,
now and in all eternity.
Amen.

Collect for Easter Day, *Alternative Service Book*

Most merciful God,
who by the death and resurrection of your Son Jesus Christ
delivered and saved mankind;
grant that by faith in him who suffered on the cross,
we may triumph in the power of his victory;
through Jesus Christ our Lord.
Amen.

Collect for Lent 5, *Alternative Service Book*

4 Not a new Leaf— A New Life!

God's rescue is not confined to the past. He is not concerned simply to forge a way back into his company for rebels like us. He is concerned about what happens after that. A holy God is deeply interested in the behaviour of his people. And just as he did not leave us alone to struggle towards him in our alienation so he does not leave us alone to struggle with our failings in our daily lives. His offer to every Christian believer is nothing less than his Holy Spirit. He does not expect us to turn over a new leaf: he knows how unsatisfactory that always is. He offers us a new life—a share in his own.

It's quite important to understand that God does not give us particular gifts, like a Father Christmas handing out Christmas presents. He gives us himself. For he is love, and love does not hold back. Love gives all for the beloved. Amazingly, he loves us that much. He gives us himself in that great rescue of which we read in the last two chapters. He did that to put us right with him. And in the Holy Spirit he gives us himself so that he can keep us right with him. Our God is a supreme giver.

John records some marvellous teaching by Jesus about the Holy Spirit, given on the last night of his life, as he celebrated the Passover in that Upper Room. There is not a lot about the Holy Spirit in the Gospels—probably because God's Holy Spirit, active in many ways in Old Testament times, was concentrated in the person of Jesus while he was on earth. But now, as he is about to die, Jesus wants his followers to know they are not going to be left like desolate orphans. He has a wonderful parting gift to leave for them, the Spirit which has so manifestly indwelt him.

'If you love me you will obey what I command. And I will ask the Father, and he will give you another Counsellor to be with you for ever—the Spirit of truth. The world cannot accept him, because it neither sees him nor knows him. But you know him, for he lives with you, and will be in you. I will not leave you as orphans; I will come to you. Before long, the world will not see me any more but you will see me. Because I live, you also will live. On that day you will realise that I am in my Father, and you are in me, and I in you. Whoever has my commands and obeys them, he is the one who loves me. He who loves me will be loved by my Father and I too will love him and show myself to him.'

Then Judas (not Judas Iscariot) said, 'But, Lord, why do you intend to show yourself to us and not to the world?' Jesus replied, 'If anyone loves me, he will obey my teaching. My Father will love him, and we will come to him and make our home with him. He who does not love me will not obey my teaching. These words you hear are not my own; they belong to the Father who sent me. All this I have spoken while still with you. But the Counsellor, the Holy Spirit, whom the Father will send in my name, will teach you all things and will remind you of everything

I have said to you. Peace I leave with you; my peace I give you. I do not give to you as the world gives. Do not let your hearts be troubled, and do not be afraid.'

John 14:15–27

Do you begin to see a bit more clearly the nature of this God who has come to our rescue? First, he shows himself as the God *over* us—the Holy One, the Creator, the Only. Then he shows himself to us as the God *alongside* us—in the person, the dying and rising of Jesus. And the third stage in his self-disclosure is that this same God can come and live *within* us, progressively enabling us to approximate to the lifestyle of Jesus. God over us, God alongside us, God in us.

The doctrine of the Trinity is not there to bemuse us, but because that's how it is with the great God we worship—over us, alongside us, within us. So you could properly say that the Holy Spirit is that aspect of the Godhead whose supreme function is to indwell believers, just as he indwelt Jesus during the days of his flesh. See again the overwhelming generosity of God. He gives us not just a gift, but himself. He does not simply call on us to turn over a new leaf. He offers us his new life!

This passage in John's Gospel is deceptively simple in the language it uses but it is very profound in its teaching. We cannot hope to plumb it here, but there are a number of important indications which Jesus gives to tell us who the Spirit is and what he is intended to do in our lives.

First, the Spirit is personal. No vague influence, but the unseen yet intensely living and personal God. A 'he', not an 'it'. Church language about 'the Holy Ghost' may have obscured that important truth for us. And it is important. A personal God offers us nothing less than his personal presence, his Spirit.

Secondly, the Spirit is a gift. He is not to be earned or bartered for. He is the Father's love gift to us. Just as our forgiveness is a free gift from a loving God, so is the Holy Spirit. 'The world' (society which leaves God out of account) 'cannot accept him, because it neither sees him nor knows him.' A materialistic outlook, common in our society today as then, simply cannot understand this unseen Spirit of God, who cannot be seen or measured. But he is real, and he is the Father's precious gift to us.

Thirdly, the Spirit will not be withdrawn. He will be 'with you for ever'. In Old Testament days the Spirit might be given to a King Saul or a Samson—and removed because of human sin. Jesus promises the unwithdrawn presence of the Spirit for ever. We may grieve him when we do wrong. But we do not drive him away. He is with us for keeps.

Fourthly, the Spirit comes to live within us. 'He lives *with* you,' says Jesus. They knew something of his grace and power living with them—in the person of their Master. But now that he was about to die, that same Spirit would be released from the confines of the body of Jesus to come and literally live within the hearts of believers. He 'will be *in* you'.

It began on the day of Pentecost. That glorious chapter of history has never come to an end—and it never will until the end of time. No wonder Paul can say, 'If anyone does not have the Spirit of Christ, he does not belong to Christ' (Romans 8:9). The fundamental definition of a Christian is someone who has received the Spirit into his or her life. No wonder this is seen as a new birth, or life from above. Instead of working on us from outside, the Spirit of God is now released within us to change us from inside.

Fifthly, the Spirit makes Jesus real to us. 'I will come to you . . . you will realise that I am in my Father, and you are in me, and I am in you.' 'I too will love him and show myself to him.' It is the task of the Holy Spirit to make Jesus real to us. No longer a stained-glass window figure of history, but a constant companion and friend. It is the Spirit who makes Jesus our contemporary. He does it in much the same way as Jesus made the unseen God contemporary. Jesus describes his relationship with his Father as a mutual indwelling. The Father lives in him, and he in the Father. And it is something like that with the Christian. Now that the Spirit is given to us, we live in the Spirit and the Spirit lives in us and makes Jesus vibrantly alive to us.

Sixthly, the Holy Spirit brings us assurance. He makes us clear that we belong. 'You know him . . . you will see me . . . you will live.' There is a wonderful touch of immediacy here. We are meant to know we belong. To be sure, we have a terribly long way to go in the Christian life, but the Spirit is the one given to assure us that we really do belong. Without the foundation of that assurance it would be very difficult to construct the building of a Christian life. And there is nothing arrogant about this quiet assurance. Remember, it's a gift! Paul was very clear on this when he wrote, 'You received the Spirit of sonship. And by him we cry, "Abba, Father." The Spirit himself testifies with our spirit that we are God's children. Now if we are children, then we are heirs—heirs of God and co-heirs with Christ' (Romans 8:15–17).

There's a further aspect of the Spirit's coming which shines out of this passage in John. He makes us feel at home with God. Jesus does not only say that the Spirit will come to the believer. He does not only say the Spirit will make his own presence real to the believer. He says that through the Spirit the whole Godhead will come and make their home in the believer. Staggering thought. But that is what he says. 'My Father will love him, and we will come to him and make our home with him.' No longer the God from whom we shrink in discomfort, if not fear. This God is our God for ever. He has come to make his home with us. He does not restrict his presence to churches: 'Do you not know that your body is a temple of the Holy Spirit, who is in you, whom you have received from God?' (1 Corinthians 6:19).

An eighth aspect of the Holy Spirit in our lives is that he teaches us and reminds us. 'The Counsellor . . . will teach you all things, and will remind you of everything I have said to you.' The very name 'Counsellor' points to that role, though it is a complicated word with legal associations: he is both prosecuting counsel when we stray, and defending counsel to comfort and encourage. This 'counselling' function the Spirit has fulfilled partly by reminding the apostles of what Jesus had taught and enabling them to write it down for us in the New Testament; and partly by enlivening and illuminating our conscience so that we are more sensitive to pleasing Jesus in daily life, and doing what he would want us to. He teaches us through Scripture. And he teaches us through that quiet inner voice which we increasingly learn to recognize and, if we are wise, to obey.

Ninthly, the Spirit brings peace to our troubled hearts. 'Peace I leave with you; my peace I give you. I do not give to you as the world gives. Do not let your hearts be troubled and do not be afraid.' What a marvellous promise! We all have troubles. We all have fears. But Jesus says that it is wrong, actually sinful, to give in to them. We should consciously hand them over to the Holy Spirit and ask him to bring his peace over us, the peace that sustained Jesus even on that terrible evening when he knew the cross was beckoning. Peace is meant to mark Christians: the world certainly does not give peace! And we cannot create it in ourselves. It is the work of the indwelling Spirit to realize Jesus' own peace in us. He does so as we commit the situation to him.

And finally, the Spirit enables loving obedience to grow in us. There is a constant interweaving, in these words of Jesus, between loving obedience to him keeping his commandments, on the one hand; and the power and guidance of the indwelling Spirit, on the other. They belong together. The Spirit is not given to make us comfortable, but to make us like Jesus—something which, by nature, we cannot be. We can only turn over a new leaf each New Year's Day: and it is spoiled within a day or two! The Spirit is given us to enable a new life which grows more and more like Christ until the day when we meet him face to face, at the end of the road.

Praise God for the gift of the Holy Spirit, the birthright of every believer.

Group material, meditation and prayers

A prayer for the Decade of Evangelism from the Church in Australia:

> *Father, pour out your Spirit upon your people,*
> *and grant to us:*
> *a new vision of your glory;*
> *a new faithfulness to your Word;*
> *a new consecration to your service;*
> *that your life may grow among us,*
> *and your kingdom come;*
> *through Jesus Christ our Lord.*
> *Amen.*

Slowly, read out the passage near the beginning of this chapter, John 14:15–27. Then discuss the following questions:

1. How would you best explain in a single sentence who the Holy Spirit is to someone to whom the whole idea is new and strange?

46

2. Is it wrong to be sure that you have received the Holy Spirit into your life?

3. What difference has he made to you? What difference is he meant to make?

4. Why is the Holy Spirit such an important part of Christianity?

Meditation

Please will you all close your eyes, and sit in the way that is most comfortable for you. It seems to be best for meditation to sit up, with your back straight—but not tense. Let your feet be flat on the floor—and let your hands rest on your knees. Now relax for a few moments, and become aware of your breathing . . .

The Spirit of God is the breath of God. Your breathing can be a symbol of the Spirit for you. As you breathe in the life-giving oxygen in the air think of God as the source of your life—always there for you. Now remember Jesus with the disciples after the resurrection.

> On the evening of that first day of the week, when the disciples were together, with the doors locked for fear of the Jews, Jesus came and stood among them and said, 'Peace be with you!' After he said this, he showed them his hands and side. The disciples were overjoyed when they saw the Lord. Again Jesus said, 'Peace be with you! As the Father has sent me, I am sending you.' And with that he breathed on them and said, 'Receive the Holy Spirit.'
>
> John 20:19–22

Now suggest that people pray aloud as they feel moved to do so, prayers that arise from the discussion, and prayers for particular people.

Final prayers

Sing this well-known chorus quietly as a prayer:

Spirit of the living God, fall afresh on me.
Spirit of the living God, fall afresh on me.
Break me, melt me, mould me, fill me,
Spirit of the living God, fall afresh on me.

Almighty God,
who at this time
taught the hearts of your faithful people
by sending to them the light of your Holy Spirit;
grant to us by the same Spirit
to have right judgement in all things,
and evermore to rejoice in his holy comfort;
through the merits of Christ Jesus our Saviour,
who is alive and reigns with you in the unity of the Spirit,
one God, now and for ever.
Amen.

Collect for Pentecost, *Alternative Service Book*

---

5   Wholehearted Response

The Christian life offers all—and demands all. God, the great Lover of mankind, has put his life at stake for us, given all for us, and has the right to ask for our wholehearted response. When it is not forthcoming, it breaks his heart. And this is what he revealed to John on Patmos in a famous passage in the Book of Revelation.

To the angel of the church in Laodicea write: These are the words of the Amen, the faithful and true witness, the ruler of God's creation. I know your deeds, that you are neither cold nor hot. I wish you were either one or the other! So, because you are lukewarm—neither hot nor cold—I am about to spit you out of my mouth. You say 'I am rich; I have acquired wealth and do not need a thing.' But you do not realise that you are wretched, pitiful, poor, blind, and naked. I counsel you to buy from me gold refined in the fire, so that you can become rich; and white clothes to wear, so that you can cover your shameful nakedness; and salve to put on your eyes, so that you can see. Those whom I love I rebuke and discipline. So be earnest, and repent. Here I am! I stand at the door and knock. If anyone hears my voice and opens the door, I will come in and eat with him, and he with me.

Revelation 3:14–20

This is a particularly instructive passage of Scripture. We notice that it is written not to atheists or to some anti-Christian movement, but to a church, the church at Laodicea. The writer clearly knows it well. His allusions are very apt. For Laodicea was a rich city, situated at the junction of the north-south and the east-west trade routes of Asia Minor (Turkey).

It was a celebrated banking centre. It was also well known for the jackets made there from glossy-coated black sheep: they were much prized. Nearby was a medical school which specialized in the care of the eyes. And the city itself, though flourishing and splendidly built, had one great handicap. There was no water supply. It had to be brought by pipes from miles away. By the time it arrived it was lukewarm, and revolting. Indeed, the citizens would sometimes use it as an emetic in a big feast to make themselves sick so that they could eat another few courses!

These local characteristics seem to have rubbed off on the church, founded, no doubt, like Colossae next door, during the big expansion of Christianity from the great city of Ephesus during the fifties. Paul, you will remember, held forth daily in the School of Tyrannus 'so that all the Jews and Greeks who lived in the province of Asia heard the word of the Lord' (Acts 19:10).

By the nineties, when John received this message from the ascended Christ which he sent as a letter to Laodicea, it is apparent that all was far from well with the church. Jesus is the 'faithful and true witness', and he deals very straight with them. These churchmen are lukewarm, like the revolting local water supply. And it makes the Lord sick. He is about to spit them out of his mouth.

Strong language, indeed. But justified. They think, as many in our churches think, that all is well. The church is reasonably well filled.

The service is well taken. The music is beautiful. The bills are paid. The people are civilized. What could possibly be lacking? The situation is so very contemporary that it would be well worth finding out.

Let us see how Jesus handles this problem. He does it in four stages.

First, his **diagnosis**. He helps them to see what they are really like, and they find this very difficult. They are successful people in the world's eyes, and they maintain, 'I am rich. I have acquired wealth, and do not need a thing.' No doubt they are right, humanly speaking. But Jesus cannot be taken in, and he cannot be bought off. He is the one with laser vision who knows their deeds. And what he sees is distressing in the extreme. They are 'wretched', despite their wealth. They are 'pitiful' in their attempts to show off and tell God what great people they are. They are 'poor', despite their merchant banks, 'blind', despite their medical school, and 'naked', despite their celebrated fleeces. They have a lot of things with which to impress one another— but nothing to impress God. He sees through the shallow exterior to the empty heart inside. Such is the diagnosis of the sickness by the Great Physician. And the tragic thing is that they 'do not realise'.

Secondly comes Jesus' **offer**. It is very wonderful. He promises them a complete cure, if they are willing for what it takes. He is the one who has the true spiritual riches: the riches of character, of love, moral power, unselfishness and the rest. He offers them white clothes to wear, so that they can cover their shameful nakedness. What he means is that for all their vaunted finery, they are not fit to be seen before God. They have nothing to wear. Their clothes of imagined goodness are moth-eaten. As Isaiah had said long ago, even their 'righteous acts are like filthy rags' (Isaiah 64:6) before the blazing purity of God. Their expensive black cloaks will avail them nothing. But Jesus is willing and able to clothe them in the white garments of his own perfect goodness. Had he not taken their filthy garments and worn them on the cross— for sinners like them, and like us?

Then Jesus longs for us to accept, as a sheer gift, the perfect standing before God which is his by right. In the imagery here it is seen as a spotless robe to wear at the divine party! And that was a very influential metaphor in the New Testament, which has a lot to say about us being 'clothed' in Christ, putting on the Lord Jesus Christ, and being 'in Christ'. So here Jesus offers those proud Laodiceans his own goodness to wear before God. And to round it off, he offers them eye-salve which they could never get from their medical school: it will give them a new vision, and the clear sight to see themselves, to see Jesus, and to see the needy world around them and realize what they can do to serve it. Such was his offer. That offer stands today.

But notice, thirdly, his **challenge**. Jesus tells them to take the matter very seriously. We can understand that. He tells them to repent and change their attitude. That too makes sense. But now we come to the heart of both his offer and his challenge. It is this. Jesus tells these churchgoers that for all their church attendance, for all their respectability, he has never been given personal access to their individual lives or to their church at large. They represent a Christless church! He is the one who can meet their needs, but they have never let him do it. They have kept him out.

These people look like Christians on the outside but if you scratch them you will find unchanged human nature underneath. They give God an hour on Sundays, but don't want to reckon with him for the rest of the week. Above all, they are self-satisfied. They have never done anyone any harm. Their lives are better than most. 'I am rich, I have acquired wealth, I do not need a thing.' It is that attitude of proud self-sufficiency that keeps Christ at bay. He cannot give them what they need—the true riches, the right standing before God, the spiritual insight—until they allow him to come in. He stands outside and waits for a response.

You may know Holman Hunt's famous picture of Jesus standing outside the door of a dark cottage and knocking. His robe is spotless white. His cloak is blood red. His hands bear the scars of the nails. His head is crowned with thorns. He holds a lantern: is he not the Light of the world? Ivy grows up the door. It has clearly never been opened.

That house represents our life. Jesus made the house. Jesus purchased it back at tremendous cost when it had been illegally seized by me, the tenant. He has a double right to come in. But there is no handle visible on the door in the picture. When asked about that detail, the artist responded, 'The handle is on the inside.' It is indeed. And patiently the Saviour waits until he is invited in.

It is a very simple step. You know how to ask someone into your house? Then you know how to invite Jesus to come by his Spirit and enter your life. It is a very necessary step. With Jesus excluded, this church at Laodicea could never grow and come alive. It is vital to invite him in. And notice what a personal step it is. It is the church which is lukewarm; the church which fancies itself but is so empty. Yet this situation cannot be remedied *en masse*. Jesus gently faces every individual in that church and says, 'Here I am! I stand at the door and knock.'

Amazing that he should wait there so patiently until I in my pride and selfishness humble myself enough to invite him in. He knocks— incredible that he should want to come into a house such as mine. 'If anyone hears my voice,' he says . . . Why, yes, I've heard him gently challenging me on this very personal matter of response. I have realized that though I have been brought up in the Church I have never personally invited Christ to come and take his proper place in my heart and life.

So what must I do? Why, 'open the door.' And how do I do that? Simply by praying, 'Lord, please come in. I've not realized it before but I've never asked you in. I've kept you out all these years. Please come in and start reconstructing and redecorating this house of mine.' What does Jesus say? *'I will come in.'* If we ask him, he will come. And our lives will not become dreary and narrow, as we rather fear if we start taking Jesus seriously. He offers us life in all its fullness and it will be a feast. 'I will come in and eat with him, and he with me'—the oriental image of close and lasting friendship.

We only need to take this step of surrender and inviting Christ into our life once. It never needs to be repeated, although we shall often have to come back and confess some failure and ask his pardon. That is a regular part of Christian living. But we never need to ask him in again. For when he comes, his promise is: 'Never will I leave you; never will I forsake you' (Hebrews 13:5). I may often let him down. I may often be a very poor disciple. But I *am* a disciple. He has come in, and he will not leave me. I need to grow in the friendship and the discipleship that are just beginning in this personal way. But I do not need to keep on asking him in again. That step, of course, is not the end—but it is the end of the beginning.

Before we leave this very important matter, notice the fourth thing to which Jesus draws attention. Not only our need; not only what he can do for us; not only the vital importance of inviting him to share life with us; but the **confidence** that begins to grow from that step of faith. 'I will come in,' he says. No doubt about it. He cannot break his word.

And come in he does. 'I will eat with him'—and companionship and joy will become something of a reality.

And then Jesus points to the overcoming life, a life which can face hardship and opposition, that can sail through storms and survive in long dark nights of the soul. He says, 'To him who overcomes, I will give the right to sit with me on my throne just as I overcame and sat down with my Father on his throne.'

Jesus is making it very plain that the decision to come and follow him is the best and most critical decision we ever make. Have you made it yet? I know that for many years I moved in church circles, and sometimes read my Bible, but had no idea that a personal relationship with Jesus Christ lay at the heart of the Christian life. Let alone that it was possible! I thank God for the day he bought me to my knees. I asked Jesus to come by his Spirit into my life. And it was the beginning of something entirely new: a wholehearted response to wholehearted love.

Group material, meditation and prayers

A prayer of Ignatius Loyola:

> Lord, take over all the remaining years of my life. Take my understanding, take my will, all that I am and all that I possess. It is thou who hast given them. To thee I hand them back entire. And henceforth to thy will and guidance I surrender. Give me in return deep love of thee, and with it give thy gracious strength. Then I am rich enough, and ask no more.

Have a short silence of a couple of minutes after the prayer. Then ask people to turn to Revelation 3:14–20 in their Bibles (the passage at the start of this chapter). Read it out and then discuss the following questions.

1. Is this personal response to Christ a necessity for all Christians, or an option for some?

2. Why do many churches seem to lack fire and personal enthusiasm?

3. How does this personal response to Christ relate to baptism and confirmation?

Meditation

People will find this more useful for reflection if you leave good spaces in between the phrases.

Please shut your eyes and settle yourself in your chair. Put your back against the back of the chair, and your feet flat on the floor, and your hands on your knees. Then just relax. Be aware of yourself, sitting here. Then be aware of other people around you. Remember the promise of Jesus: 'Where two or three are gathered together in my name, there I am in the midst of them.'

So Jesus is here in the midst of us, even though we can't see him. He wants to stay with us, and to live in us—in each person here, and in our church. So first of all let each one of us reflect on ourself.

Room for pleasure, room for business
But for Christ the crucified
Not a room that he can enter
In the life for which he died.

Now, in our mind's eye, let's see Jesus standing outside the door and wanting to enter in. Perhaps we've never opened the door of our heart to allow him to come in, or perhaps we have invited him in, and he's come in—but we're still keeping some rooms closed to him. He wants to come into all of them. Listen to the words of the children's song—and if you want to, use it as a prayer.

Into my heart, into my heart,
Come into my heart, Lord Jesus.
Come in today
Come in to stay.
Come into my heart, Lord Jesus.

If you invite him, he will assuredly come. Did he not promise, 'if *anyone . . .* opens the door, I *will* come in'? If you have asked him, then he *has* come in. So why not thank him for doing so—now, in your heart? Feelings and changes will follow in due course; and they come in different ways for different people. But the basic fact is that when we ask, he comes. He cannot break his word.

Now have a silence for two or three minutes, then invite people to pray their own prayers aloud if they want to.

Final prayers

A prayer for the Decade of Evangelism from the Church in the Southern Cone:

> *Loving Father, whose grace abounds towards those lost:*
> *in their poverty and wealth;*
> *in their sin and self-righteousness;*
> *in their hatred and their pride;*
> *grant that your own people may demonstrate*
> *your grace in their lives,*
> *and their joy in spite of pain;*
> *in giving with delight;*
> *in their victory over sin;*
> *in their love for all;*
> *in their humility before others,*
> *and thus commend the gospel*
> *of our Lord Jesus Christ,*
> *who lives and reigns with you and the Holy Spirit,*
> *one God, now and for ever.*
> *Amen.*

A prayer of dedication:

> *Almighty God,*
> *we thank you for the gift of your holy word.*
> *May it be a lantern to our feet,*
> *a light to our paths,*
> *and a strength to our lives.*

Take us and use us
to love and serve all men
in the power of the Holy Spirit
and in the name of your Son,
Jesus Christ our Lord. Amen.

Alternative Service Book

Thou didst leave thy throne and thy kingly crown,
When thou camest to earth for me;
But in Bethlehem's home was there found no room
For thy holy Nativity:
O come to my heart, Lord Jesus;
There is room in my heart for thee.

Emily E.S. Elliott

6

New Society

Let's be very clear about one thing. The Christianity which does not begin with the individual doesn't begin. But the Christianity which ends with the individual ends. You come through a narrow gate into the family of God all on your own, and then you discover a whole new world. You are part of a new family. You are a member of a new society. You are a limb in a world-wide body. It is unashamedly corporate.

Listen to how it was at the very beginning, on the day of Pentecost:

> With many other words Peter warned them; and he pleaded with them, 'Save yourselves from this corrupt generation.' Those who accepted his message were baptised, and about three thousand were added to their number that day. They devoted themselves to the apostles' teaching, and to the fellowship, to the breaking of bread, and to prayer. Everyone was filled with awe, and many wonders and miraculous signs were done by the apostles. All the believers were together and had everything in common. Selling their possessions and goods, they gave to anyone as he had need.

Every day they continued to meet together in the temple courts. They broke bread in their homes, and ate together with glad and sincere hearts, praising God and enjoying the favour of all the people. And the Lord added to their number daily those who were being saved.

Acts 2:40–47

That is one of Luke's descriptions of the first Church. Here is the other:

All the believers were one in heart and mind. No-one claimed that any of his possessions was his own, but they shared everything they had. With great power the apostles continued to testify to the resurrection of the Lord Jesus, and much grace was upon them all. There were no needy persons among them. For from time to time those who owned lands or houses sold them, brought the money from the sales, and put it at the apostles' feet, and it was distributed to anyone as he had need. Joseph, a Levite from Cyprus, whom the apostles called Barnabas (which means Son of Encouragement), sold a field he owned and brought the money and put it at the apostles' feet. Now a man named Ananias, together with his wife Sapphira, also sold a piece of property. With his wife's full knowledge he kept back part of the money for himself, but brought the rest and put it at the apostles' feet.

Acts 4:32—5:2

One thing is crystal clear from these two impressionist sketches of the early Christians. Nobody got the idea that they could worship God just as well in their back garden and that they did not need the fellowship of other Christians. It was a cohesive movement, it was a task force, from the very outset.

There are a number of notable marks of the Church which meet us in these two passages. They distinguished the first Christians, and they need to be part of our aims in church life today.

First, they **baptized** the new believers. Baptism, repentance and faith, and receiving the Holy Spirit are the three interwoven strands of becoming a Christian. Peter had called on his hearers not merely to repent and believe (as Protestants emphasize), or to be baptized (as

59

Catholics emphasize), or to receive the Holy Spirit (as the Pentecostals emphasize). All three belong together. If you like, Baptism is the churchly part of initiation; to repent and believe is the personal response we all need to make at some time; and the gift of the Spirit is the divine side of our initiation as Christians. All three are important. We would be very unwise to play one off against the other, as is often done. 'A threefold cord is not quickly broken' (Ecclesiastes 4:12 RSV).

The apostles' **teaching** was very important for the infant Church. And so it still is. In those days it was verbal teaching, based on the Old Testament and its fulfilment in Jesus together with the words and deeds of their Master and what the Holy Spirit was beginning to teach them. Nowadays the apostles' teaching is enshrined in the Scriptures, and summaries of scriptural teaching in the Creeds. It is important that we hold to these Christian basics and do not sacrifice them simply because the climate of the day may be unfavourable. It is noteworthy that the churches which across the world seek to be guided by the Scriptures are the ones which are strong, growing and gaining converts. Those that cut their cloth according to the latest vagaries of theological fashion tend not to attract dedicated new believers and not to change lives.

The apostles' **fellowship** was no less important. We cannot be a Christian on our own—unless we are incarcerated in prison or a desert island. The word 'fellowship' literally means 'joint participation in' and that is what real Christian fellowship is. Together we participate in worship and outreach and recreation and service because we are fellow members of the family of God. God's purpose in his great rescue act is not only to save individual souls (that is just the start of it), but to create a new society of men, women and children who have been reconciled with him and with each other, and together set out to serve others for his sake.

Holy Communion was vitally important for developing that fellowship with the ascended Lord and with each other. They made it a regular part of their lives. This is an area where Anglicans are quite strong, and have a lot to offer to some of the other churches who rarely celebrate the Communion together.

The first believers were equally dedicated in the area of **prayer**. The Christian Church has had a wonderful history of praying heroes, but in this activist and very materialistic age in which we live it is both difficult and imperative to keep prayer in the forefront of our lives. In some mysterious way which we cannot explain, but all know to be true, prayer releases the activity of God in this world. It is a 'must'.

But Luke is far from done. He points to an area of spirituality which has revived strongly among the charismatic and Pentecostal churches throughout the world but is still viewed with a good deal of suspicion among many of us. 'Many **wonders** and miraculous signs were done by the apostles,' he says. And not just by the apostles. The Acts, and the next few centuries for that matter, are full of healings, deliverance from dark forces, release from impossible circumstances and so on, which were 'signs' of God's activity among humanity and helped to wake people up to his reality. We must neither be unduly credulous on this matter nor fall into the trap of scepticism as if God had, for all practical purposes, gone out of business. This is an attitude bred by the eighteenth-century Enlightenment which is widely influential but is on the way out (and not before it is time) in this 'post-modern' era.

Sharing is another notable feature of these first Christians. They shared not only their income but their capital. They were the first to adopt the policy later taken over by the communists: 'to each according to his need; from each according to his ability.' This is the only example of such radical communalism that we find in the early Church, but there is no doubt that sharing was a way of life with them. Alas, that isn't so with us. When people see us making really free of our home, our car, washing machine and so forth for other believers, they see something which is rare in secular society. And they may well sit up and take notice. At all events we ought to be noticeably less materialistic and noticeably more generous than those who do not know our Lord. It is a benchmark of authentic Christianity.

Worship is, of course, a primary mark of the Church. And this we normally associate with church on Sunday. Well, the first Christians had a counterpart to that. They were to be found daily (mark you) meeting for worship in the temple (even though temple worship would not have been altogether to their liking, since their lives had been turned upside down by Jesus). But that was not the whole story. We find them meeting often in the Acts (and it is stressed here) in private houses. That is something which is coming in more and more these days, and not a moment too soon. Because what you lose in dignity in a home meeting you gain in intimacy; what you lose in leadership you gain in sharing. One of the best ways I know for a church to come alive is for it to grow many home meetings where Christians can meet, and share and get picked up when exhausted; where they can pool their lives and their loves, their joys and their sorrows. I know I could not now survive without some such small group as this to belong to. It is just as important as the big meetings in church.

Luke is struck by the element of **praise** which figured so prominently in the early Church. Every renewal of religion produces with it new songs of praise to the God who has become so real. It is very sad—and quite unnecessary—when church members fall out over new songs versus old hymns. There is room for both! But of one thing I am sure. Whenever the Spirit of God is strongly at work among a group of people the result is always a paean of praise going up to God the Creator and Saviour and Friend.

Another feature which appeals to Luke is the **encouragement** which Barnabas so manifestly embodied. His name, of course, was not Barnabas but Joseph. Yet everyone knows him as Barnabas, which is his nickname and means 'Encourager'. There is often a lot of strain, and sometimes backbiting, in church circles and encouragers are worth their weight in gold. It is one of God's most precious gifts to a community, and it should be a prominent characteristic of every congregation. The lovely thing is that each one of us can be an encourager if we set out to be!

I am very struck by another feature of their life. They were strong on **testimony**—in the streets, in people's homes, and among friends. They were not slow to come out with what God had done for them through the Messiah Jesus. They were not in the least embarrassed to talk about Jesus. They did not preach. They intrigued! That is what a witness does. He does not argue or pontificate. He simply tells what his experience has been. And it is very powerful. We do not so much need lots of electrifying preachers in the churches (what good is a preacher if few come to hear him?). We do need every church member to turn into a witness. And that would revolutionize the impact of the Church on society.

It certainly did in the early days. We read that people approved of these followers of Jesus. They enjoyed the **favour** of all the people—I suppose they stood out in such striking contrast to the earthbound, ecclesiastical Sadducees and the often priggish Pharisees. They loved Jesus and loved people. And that is still a sure-fire prescription for growth.

And **growth** is precisely what happened. There are many countries in Africa which have the same problem as these first Christians in the Acts. They have too many converts. The Lord is adding to their number daily those who are being saved. In the West this is much more rare, but it still happens at times. I have known such times occasionally in my own ministry: people coming to knock on the door and asking, in effect, how to become Christians! I wish it happened more often. I guess it would if our church life learnt a little from the joy, the sacrifice, the commitment and the fellowship of the first disciples of Jesus and those they brought to faith.

But there is one other mark of the Church. It is always present, and (lest we should get too starry-eyed an impression of the earliest Church) Luke is careful to record it. You will always find sin and **failure** in the Church—as in the case of Annanias and Sapphira. The Church is the school for sinners, not the society of the perfect. The great nineteenth-century preacher Charles Spurgeon gave some excellent advice to a woman seeking the perfect church. 'You won't find it,' he told her 'and if you do don't join it. If you do, you will only spoil it!'

Group material, meditation and prayers

A prayer for the Decade of Evangelism from the Church in Sabah:

> *Gracious Father, we pray that you will bless the work of your Church during this Decade of Evangelism, and that you will prosper our efforts on its behalf. Equip and send forth labourers into the fields and provide them with the means of their support. Grant that we may take our share in the work by our prayers, our service and our gifts, to the glory of your Name, the salvation of souls and the building up of the Body of Christ. And fill us with the spirit of self-sacrifice, for the sake of him who suffered and died for us, thy Son our Saviour Jesus Christ. Amen.*

When you have finished the prayer, have a brief silence for one or two minutes. Then slowly read out the two passages from Acts at the start of this chapter, 2:40–47 and 4:32—5:2, and discuss the following questions.

1. Why is it not possible to be a Christian all on your own?

2. Why does the Church today in the West so often lack dynamism?

3. Why have young people, by and large, voted with their feet against the Church?

4. Which of those qualities in the early Church do you see in your own congregation? And which are missing?

Meditation

Turn in your Bibles to 1 Corinthians chapters 12 and 13. Divide the chapters up into as many sections as there are people (including whoever is leading the group this week) and then read round. After each person has finished let there be a pause for reflection before the next person starts. It might be helpful if the leader gives a nod to each person to indicate when they are to begin, since some people find waiting and silences hard to handle.

Finish with a time of open prayer.

Final prayers

Lord, we pray for the spread of the gospel.
Bless those who preach, teach, heal, build, reconcile, bring hope,
that their message may be the means of salvation to those who
hear;
and grant that your church may grow and increase in the
knowledge of your divine love.

Reproduced from *Further Everyday Prayers* edited by Hazel Snashall with the permission of the National Christian Education Council. Taken from *The Lion Prayer Collection*

Almighty Father,
whom truly to know is eternal life;
teach us to know your Son Jesus Christ
as the way, the truth and the life;
that we may follow the steps
of your holy apostles Philip and James
and walk steadfastly in the way that leads to your glory;
through Jesus Christ our Lord.

Collect for St Philip and St James, Apostles

Finish by saying the Grace together, and suggest that everyone keeps their eyes open, and looks round at other people as they pray this final prayer.

The grace of our Lord Jesus Christ, and the love of God, and the
fellowship of the Holy Spirit be with us all evermore. Amen.

Part Two

Six Bible Studies on How to Share the Christian Faith

Introduction

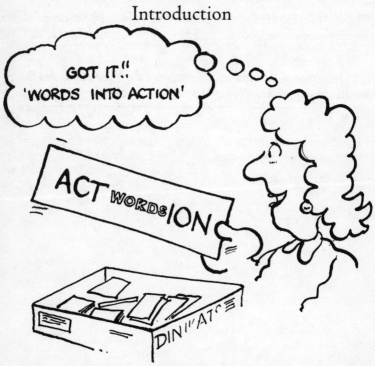

In the first six studies, I have deliberately moved from book to book of the Bible. Despite the diversity of the authors, the message of the Bible has a profound unity. It does not much matter where you turn. The same great themes of God and man, love and forgiveness, sin and righteousness, salvation and discipleship, emerge.

But in the second part of this little book, I have chosen all the passages from the Acts of the Apostles. I do this partly because it is the only account we possess of how this tiny handful of men and women turned into a movement which captured and survived the great Roman Empire. We have no other source to turn to until well into the second century.

I do it partly because I believe we have so much to learn from the way those early Christians went about their task of evangelism. Despite the profound cultural differences between their day and ours, despite two thousand years of history, we have so much to learn from them if we want to reach our compatriots in our day with the eternal gospel.

And I do it partly—yes I confess it—because I love the Acts and find myself drawn back to it again and again.

So let us see what those men and women did *in their day* to spread the good news; and then decide whether that offers us any directions as we begin *now* the task of re-evangelizing the once-Christian world, no less. We cannot, of course, go direct from page to action: but we can, I believe, gain much inspiration and insight from the way these intrepid disciples set about winning society to the allegiance of their Lord Jesus.

7 Sharing the Faith Through Church Life

It has got to begin here. If our 'product' is unattractive, nobody will want it. If our church life is not appealing we shall get nowhere in evangelism. The church life of the first-century Christians seems to have been very attractive indeed. Here is just one example that is a favourite of mine. Luke tells us about the founding of the church at Antioch: a vast, 'modern' city in Syria, rivalling Rome and Alexandria in population and splendour.

Now those who had been scattered by the persecution in connection with Stephen travelled as far as Phoenicia, Cyprus and Antioch, telling the message only to Jews. Some of them, however, men from Cyprus and Cyrene, went to Antioch and began to speak to Greeks also, telling them the good news about the Lord Jesus. The Lord's hand was with them, and a great mumber of people believed and turned to the Lord. News of this reached the ears of the church at Jerusalem, and they sent Barnabas to Antioch. When he arrived, and saw the evidence of the grace of God, he was glad and encouraged them all to remain true to the Lord with all their hearts. He was a good man, full of the Holy Spirit and faith, and a great number of people were brought to the Lord.

Then Barnabas went to Tarsus to look for Saul, and when he found him he brought him to Antioch. So for a whole year Barnabas and Saul met with the church and taught great numbers of people. The disciples were called Christians first at Antioch. During this time some prophets came down from Jerusalem to Antioch. One of them, named Agabus, stood up and through the Spirit predicted that a severe famine would spread over the entire Roman world. (This happened during the reign of Claudius.) The disciples, each according to his ability, decided to provide help for the brothers living in Judea. This they did, sending their gift to the elders by Saul and Barnabas.

In the church at Antioch there were prophets and teachers: Barnabas, Simeon called Niger, Lucius of Cyrene, Manaen (who had been brought up with Herod the tetrarch) and Saul. While they were worshipping the Lord and fasting, the Holy Spirit said, 'Set apart for me Barnabas and Saul for the work to which I have called them.' So, after they had fasted and prayed, they placed their hands on them and sent them off.

Acts 11:19–30; 13:1–3

How do you crack a big tough secular city like Antioch? Not by a massive ten year plan or injecting millions, but by means of a group of people aflame with love for Jesus Christ. That Antioch church became a model in many ways, and—as we attempt to pierce secular modern cities with the gospel—it still is. A number of things stand out.

First, there is the readiness to accept **change**. This church was founded as so many in Acts were, by the Hellenists. They were the friends of Stephen, and they maintained that God was always on the move, and not tied to the book, the customs, or the temple of Israel. This was bold stuff, very unattractive to the Twelve who stayed back in Jerusalem. But it was this willingness to sit light to the book, not to be over-bothered about buildings and to change 'what we did last year' which kept these early Christians vibrant, inventive and successful in their outreach. It is perhaps our reluctance to accept change which is one of our biggest handicaps in evangelism these days.

Secondly, I see it was a **lay initiative**. These informal missionaries were not ordained. They had been ejected from Jerusalem in the fracas following Stephen's death (Acts 8:1, 4). And now, without homes and without jobs, they had no thought except to tell others about the Jesus who meant so much to them. When lay initiative like that is encouraged in the Church there is always impact. The policy of 'leave it to the vicar' is the recipe for decline.

Thirdly, they were not embarrassed to **talk about Jesus**. He was 'good news' to them, and they reckoned he should be good news to other people. So they told them, naturally and enthusiastically. It is not difficult to enthuse about anything that means a lot to us. So why is it that we find it so difficult to talk about Jesus? We need to learn again from the churches in Africa and Latin America, of Singapore and Korea, where the name of Jesus is so often on the lips of believers. Jesus is, so to speak, the only card in our pack, yet we often discard him as if he were the Joker! Until ordinary Christians in the Western Church get back to talking openly about Jesus, there will be no advance.

This account teaches me the importance of **good training**. The Antioch church did not simply revel in the numbers of people joining them. They made sure there was proper training. Barnabas and Saul spent a year teaching and training them. How important that is! The modern church is weak in training. Many people get no training at all after confirmation at an early age. The sermon is depised and home study groups are still not common. Nor is training for marriage, for evangelism, for leadership of home groups, for youth work, and for particular ministries to reach particular people. No wonder the lay members of the Church imagine that all that is required of them is to come to church! If you want to evangelize, equip the laity.

This Antioch church had many other qualities from which we can learn. For one thing, they had a **shared leadership**. There was no single 'vicar' or 'bishop' at Antioch. There was a leadership team of

70

five. They were international and interracial. And that spoke volumes. Too many of our churches suffer from a 'cork in the bottle' mentality: nothing can happen without the vicar. So nothing much happens! Yet the vicar's role is to be the enabler of a leadership team which can address the many needs of the church, needs which no single person is equipped to handle (and even if they were, they wouldn't have the time).

Another unusual but important characteristic of the Antioch church is that they valued **spiritual gifts**, and were not afraid of unexpected interventions in the life of the church when the Spirit wanted to teach and direct them. One such occasion was when Agabus came down and prophesied a major famine which subsequently took place. Agabus, I guess, would not have been allowed to speak in many of our churches!

Again, the first missionary journey took place because the Church listened to the prompting of the Holy Spirit to send out two of their best leaders on this unprecedented venture. The insight probably came through a prophetic utterance by some member of the congregation. But everyone recognized that it was right and that God was in it. How would you feel if a prophecy was given in your church? Would you test it carefully—or reject it out of hand? A great many churches throughout the world show no surprise when spiritual gifts of prophecy, discernment, healing and the like take place in their midst. And life is rarely dull in such churches, though occasionally chaotic!

This leads me on to their **worship**. It was really directed to the Lord, not to each other as ours sometimes can be. It had order to it (the Greek word used for 'worshipping' here is the root of our word 'liturgy'), but it was open to the unexpected, too—in this case the indication that Saul and Barnabas should go overseas.

The Antioch church took fasting seriously, and that is something we could well emulate. Fasting opens us up to hear the God to whom we are often deaf in the bustle of a busy life. There must have been silence there, too, or they would never have discerned the Spirit's prompting about the missionary journey. Their prayer life is stressed. Nothing ever happens in evangelism without prayer, for it is not our work, but God's, to bring anyone to him. And in prayer we confess that we cannot do it, that he can, and we beg him to act.

71

There is no better way of helping our unchurched friends than to pray for them daily, and then be prepared to take such opportunities of conversation as turn up. If we had prayer like that in every church there would be a tremendous advance of the gospel our land.

The **warmth of fellowship** in this church was notable. This was the first place where Jews and Gentiles, sworn enemies, sat down to eat together as brothers and sisters in Christ. If people could see that reconciling power at work in our churches, if they could feel that warmth of welcome and love as they entered the building, if they got invited to a meal with generous hospitality afterwards, that would dispose them to listen very hard to what it was that was making such people tick.

Another very attractive quality was their **openness to human need**. As soon as they heard about the famine in Jerusalem they thought of the church there, which would have less resources than any other because they had pooled their capital as well as their income. They immediately had a collection, and they did not leave it at that; they sent it with a human face—namely Barnabas and Saul. When churches genuinely seek to meet the areas of greatest need in their locality nobody will say that the Church is irrelevant to modern life. Reaching out to society where it is hurting—that is the way of Jesus.

In all this imaginative advance they did not get arrogant and independent of other Christians. They preserved the **catholicity of the Church**. They kept in touch with Jerusalem—which was a big gesture, since the Jerusalem leaders had made no effort join them when they had first set out on their missionary travels. Yet the cohesion of the universal Church was strengthened—and that is important.

Finally, I cannot fail to notice that the disciples were for the first time called '**Christians**' here in Antioch. It was not their name for themselves, but a nickname given them by others. They were always talking about Christ. They clearly loved Christ very much. They were enthusiasts for Christ. They were dedicated to Christ. 'Right, let's call them "Christians." ' It must have happened something like that. And when churches and individuals are inflamed with love for Christ—a love which is always looking outwards—the good news will be seen to be as good and as fresh today as it was in Antioch long ago. If we want to spread the gospel, our church life is the place to start.

Group material, meditation and prayers

A prayer for the Decade of Evangelism from the Church in the West Indies:

> *O Lord God, you have called your Church to witness for you in this world. Help us to publish the good news not only in word so that everyone can understand, but also by our deeds of love. Give us the strength and courage always to stand up for righteousness, justice and peace, and may what we do now and during the Decade of Evangelism be a blessing to all, especially the poor, the powerless, the oppressed, the sick and indeed those who do not know Christ as Saviour, Liberator, Healer and the Giver of the abundant Life, for we ask it all in His Name. Amen.*

Follow that prayer with a one or two minute silence. Then read out slowly the passages from Acts 11 and 13 at the start of this chapter, and ask people to imagine the scene as they listen, either with their eyes open or shut, but seeing the scene inside their heads. Then turn to Acts 11 and 13 and discuss the following questions. It would be helpful for one person to note down any ideas which could be useful to your church as you share the good news with the people round you.

1.   What do you think are the main characteristics of the life of your local church?

2.   Where could your church profitably learn from the Antioch Christians?

3.   What are the local points of need in your society? How could the church attempt to meet some of them?

4.   What are the three biggest things that you could aim for in your church, if you long to spread the gospel locally?

Meditation

Sit comfortably and shut your eyes. Pray and think, and ask God to give you some ideas for your church, and for you. Imagine how things could be, and how you would like them to be (if they aren't like that already). Stay in silence doing this meditation for five to ten minutes.

Then spend some time going round the group and asking each person to share very briefly any new idea which they have had.

Then have a time of open prayer.

Final prayers

Our Father, your voice has called us
You have placed your name on our lips
And your work in our hands.
We are your church, your pilgrim people,
We ask you to open up for us
A future that is new.
Make us poor and make us simple,
The better to know your gospel
And to follow Jesus.
We ask your forgiveness for our past faults,
For the pride which has often driven your church
To possess itself of power.
Forgive your church if sometimes
It has not been worthy of your trust.
We are not bringing your peace to this world
Nor your salvation
To men and women divided and distressed
For we ourselves are disunited.
May we who are often divided be able
To be aware of so much that is madness
And always to seek for unity.

From the *Vocational Prayer Book* of the seminaries of the Roman Catholic Church in Spain
Taken from *The Lion Prayer Collection*

8 Sharing the Faith Through an Address

Christianity is, by definition, a missionary faith. And therefore its message has got to be heard. This, after all, is how it all began. A street demonstration in Jerusalem. An outburst of tongues. An amazed audience. And a bold preacher. You recall how it was:

'We hear them declaring the wonders of God in our own tongues.' Amazed and perplexed they asked one another, 'What does this mean?' Some, however, made fun of them and said, 'They have had too much wine.' Then Peter stood up with the Eleven, raised his voice and addressed the crowd: 'Fellow Jews and all of you who live in Jerusalem, let me explain this to you; listen carefully to what I say. These men are not drunk, as you suppose. It's only nine in the morning! No, this is what was spoken by the prophet Joel . . .'

'Men of Israel, listen to this: Jesus of Nazareth was a man accredited by God to you by miracles, wonders and signs . . . as you yourselves know. This man was handed over to you by God's set purpose and foreknowledge; and you, with the help of wicked men, put him to death by nailing him to the cross. But God raised him from the dead, freeing him from the agony of death, because it was impossible for death to keep its hold on him . . . Therefore let all Israel be assured of this: God has made this Jesus, whom you crucified, both Lord and Christ.'

When the people heard this, they were cut to the heart and said to Peter and the other apostles, 'Brothers, what shall we do?' Peter replied, 'Repent and be baptised, every one of you, in the name of Jesus Christ for the forgiveness of your sins. And you will receive the gift of the Holy Spirit. The promise is for you and your children and for all who are far off—for all whom the Lord our God will call' . . . He pleaded with them, 'Save yourselves from this corrupt generation.'

Acts 2:11–16, 22–24, 36–40

Our outreach addresses cannot be reproductions of this first and most effective sermon. But we can learn a good deal from it. Here are some of the lessons which I see in it, as someone who attempts to proclaim the good news of Jesus.

First, I am struck by the **setting**. It is not in church. It is in the open air. I reflect that Christianity began on the streets. Jesus was the street preacher *par excellence*, and so were the apostles. I shall certainly try to make good use of the 'set piece' situation in church, but I shall not be bound to it. The open air, the city hall and the pub can all be marvellous places in which to tell the good news—when the conditions are right.

Secondly, I notice the **context**. Peter is speaking into a situation which guarantees him a hearing. He sets out to answer the question which is on everyone's lips. He is profoundly relevant. As I write, the nation is rocked by scandalous goings-on in high places. Everyone is talking about them. So it was great to hear the speaker on Radio 4's 'Thought for the Day' this morning take the issue head on and proclaim the gospel through it. He would have had an enormous audience: nobody would have switched off.

Thirdly, I notice the **preacher** himself. Not ordained. Not in church. Not in robes. Not using the accustomed forms of address. It was all rather revolutionary. But it reminds me that Christian proclamation does not need to be in church, by a clergyman, properly vested, at the hallowed hour of 11.00 am. Much of the best evangelistic preaching today is done by sportsmen, arts celebrities, politicians, and business people who love Jesus and are prepared to stand up and be counted for him.

Fourthly, I cannot help being struck by Peter's **forthrightness** and **humour**. Nothing dry and mealy mouthed about him. Humorously and devastatingly he banishes their suggestion that the excited disciples were drunk. 'Not possible—the pubs aren't open.' And then, when he has them laughing with him, he tells them the unwelcome truth about themselves. It was not just the Romans who crucified Jesus: the Jewish nation was implicated too. Indeed *they* were all implicated. He was not afraid to bring them to face their own guilt. Many preachers today shy away from that. Why, important people in the church might not like it ... they might leave ... taking their big financial contribution with them.

The **content** of his address is no less striking. It is all about Jesus. Jesus the man. Jesus the divine Messiah. Jesus crucified. Jesus risen from the grave. Jesus reigning. Jesus one day coming back. And Jesus, in the meantime, sending his Holy Spirit among them—the results of which have caused such a commotion. Peter, like Paul after him, was determined to know nothing among them except Jesus, and him crucified. I do not notice that as a major characteristic of much modern preaching, even of so-called evangelistic preaching. It is weak or deficient on the person and the work of Jesus. And he is the one human hearts long for, whether they know it or not.

The **use of Scripture** is illuminating, too. Peter does not bore them by getting up and saying, 'Here begins the fourth verse of the seventeenth chapter of the Second Book of Chronicles.' He begins where they are—with their amazement over the apparent drunkenness. But during the course of his address he does show, time and again, how the Jesus events have all fallen out as the Old Testament predicted. In this way he displayed the relevance and the power of those Scriptures. Scripture does have a power that our words do not. It is, after all, inspired by the Holy Spirit, and the wise preacher finds ways in his preaching to expose people to its mighty force: but, as Peter did, in a way that intrigues, challenges and illuminates.

His **style**, too, is a striking contrast to many modern preachers, who come up with a carefully worked address smelling of the commentaries and the dictionaries and the books of quotations. Peter, of course, had not had time for such preparation, and would not have scorned it (if we may judge by the care that went into his First Epistle). But he was not the sort of man to be tied to a manuscript. Nor should the modern preacher be. Peter's example here tells me that I need to be so rooted in the Scriptures, and so enraptured with Jesus, that I can at any time speak effectively for him if the opportunity offers. Nobody is going to be helped by a twenty minute 'performance'. But they may well be moved by someone with obvious life-changing experience of Christ speaking from the heart.

Not only is Peter forthright throughout his address, he instinctively seems to know both how to **challenge** and how to **plead** with his hearers. He knows that human hearts are hard. After all, only a few weeks earlier these men had acceded to the crucifixion of the best person who ever lived. Many of them had stood and jeered as he hung dying. They need to realize the enormity of what they have done. And they need to hear the accents of Jesus gently pleading with them to change their attitude and repent, to entrust themselves to him in faith, and to be baptized into his new society. Happy the preacher who knows how to challenge and how to plead with men and women. We often fail in our preaching because we lack these finishing skills.

Finally, I am struck by the **clear explanation** Peter gives to his listeners at the end of his talk of the way to start the new life with Christ. They are to believe this message about Jesus, repent and prove it by the public sacrament of baptism. And Peter promises that the Lord Jesus will approach them with two wonderful gifts in his hands. The one is forgiveness for all the past guilt and shame, a completely fresh start. The other is his Holy Spirit, the Spirit they have already seen in other people that day, the Spirit who can come and make new people of them for the future. Peter makes it very clear to them, doesn't he? They know what they have to do. They know what to expect from Christ. They are in a position to take a decision. And three thousand of them do.

We need speakers like Peter who are very clear at the end of their address on what is being asked from the congregation. Clear, too, on what those who do respond may expect from Jesus. Alas, that clarity, that directness and simplicity is often lacking. At the end of the sermon the preacher coughs, says 'And now, to God the Father . . .' and leaves the pulpit. No, we must explain the way to faith, make clear the cost and implications of discipleship, and allow space for a prayer of response. Then, like Peter, we should expect God to have been at work—and keep a sharp eye for those who have been added to the number of believers that day, so that they can be properly looked after in the critical early stages of discipleship.

We need preachers like that.

'Oh,' you say. 'This is nothing to do with me. *I'm* not a preacher.' Yes, it is very much to do with you. You may not be a preacher. You may not be able to hold an audience in a town hall, or in a pub, or in the open air, as you speak about Jesus. But you have friends and workmates haven't you? And when you know an evangelistic event is being planned and have confidence in the speaker, you can play the invaluable part of inviting that friend or acquaintance along. We need hordes of gracious inviters! And if you have built the bridges of friendship you are more than likely to find that the person you have invited comes along. Who knows, that could be the most important meeting they ever attended—and the most important day in the whole of their life, the day they met up with Jesus.

Group material, meditation and prayers

A prayer for the Decade of Evangelism from the Episcopal Church, USA:

Almighty God, by your grace you have given us new life in Jesus Christ, and by your Spirit you have called us to proclaim his Name throughout the nations: awaken in us such a love for you and for your world that in the Decade of Evangelism we may so boldly proclaim Jesus Christ by word and deed that all people may come to know him as Saviour and follow him as Lord; to the glory of your Name. Amen.

Have a short time of silence after the prayer, and then slowly read out the passage from Acts 2 at the start of the chapter. Ask people to listen with their imagination, and to see it all happening, and to think what it must have been like on that astonishing day in Jerusalem. Some people might like to shut their eyes. Other people might like to keep their eyes open. Then ask them to turn to Acts 2 and discuss the following questions.

1. Why do you think much modern preaching is a turn-off to so many people?

2. Why do you think a lot of modern preaching has neither the zest, the conviction, nor the content of apostolic preaching?

3. Is there any place for preaching in an anti-authoritarian society where nobody listens to speeches of any kind any more?

4. What sort of qualities would you want a preacher to have if you were to invite a close friend who does not go to church to come with you?

5. Why do we hear so few laymen and laywomen speaking challengingly about Jesus nowadays?

Meditation

Please be still. Shut your eyes. Be aware of your breathing. Be aware of the chair supporting you. Be aware of other people around you—the body of Christ. The Spirit of Jesus is here with us. Now we shall be quiet for several minutes—aware of the presence of Christ in our midst, and listening to God in the quietness.

After a five or ten minute silence invite people to pray aloud. Then, after a time of prayer, ask everyone to share very briefly anything that they want to. Go all round the group, but allow people to say, 'I pass' if they don't want to speak.

Final prayers

Father, we pray for all those who preach the gospel. Thank you for all who tell out your love and grace through lives of holiness and radiant living. Help those who also try to put into words the message of hope and new life to be found in Jesus Christ. Give them the help of your Holy Spirit that their words may go straight to the minds and hearts and wills of those who hear. Through Jesus Christ our Lord. Amen.

Taken from *The Lion Prayer Collection*

A prayer for faithfulness:

Almighty God,
you have enlightened your holy Church
through the inspired witness
of your evangelist Saint Mark.
Grant that we, being firmly grounded
in the truth of the gospel,
may be faithful to its teaching
both in word and deed;
through Jesus Christ our Lord.

Collect for St Mark the Evangelist, *Alternative Service Book*

9   Sharing the Faith Through a Visit

Visiting is a long lost art. It used to be basic to every parish. But in the pressures of modern life, the increasing mobility of householders and the prevalence of working parents with latch-key kids, it has fallen into disuse. That is sad, because in the early days of the Church, and down the succeeding centuries, it proved immensely significant. Here is Luke's account of one of the most famous visits ever:

> In Damascus there was a disciple named Ananias. The Lord called him in a vision, 'Ananias!' 'Yes, Lord,' he answered. The Lord told him, 'Go to the house of Judas on Straight Street and ask for a man from Tarsus named Saul, for he is praying. In a vision he has seen a man named Ananias come and place his hands on him to restore his sight.' 'Lord,' Ananias answered, 'I have heard many reports about this man and all the harm he has done to your saints

in Jerusalem. And he has come here with authority from the chief priests to arrest all who call on your name.'

But the Lord said to Ananias, 'Go! This man is my chosen instrument to carry my name before the Gentiles and their kings and before the people of Israel. I will show him how much he must suffer for my name.' Then Ananias went to the house and entered it. Placing his hands on Saul he said, 'Brother Saul, the Lord—Jesus, who appeared to you on the road as you were coming here—has sent me so that you may see again and be filled with the Holy Spirit.' Immediately, something like scales fell from Saul's eyes, and he could see again. He got up and was baptised, and after taking some food, he regained his strength.

Acts 9:10–19

Not everyone can preach, but everyone in a congregation can visit. We never read of Ananias giving a sermon, but he did make this most important visit. He didn't want to go one little bit. He had heard the reputation of this man, Saul of Tarsus, who had an obsession for attacking and killing Christians. He was afraid—wouldn't you and I be? Ananias was the epitome of the reluctant visitor.

And yet his visit was essential. God needed Ananias to go and see Saul. And when he changed his mind and went, a wonderful discovery awaited him. He found that God had prepared the way for his visit. He found that Saul was not the man he had been. A profound change had taken place. Moreover he discovered that Saul was in great need and he was able to meet that need at a critical juncture in Saul's life. That ministry of Ananias launched Saul on the great plan God had for his life. A tremendous amount hung on Ananias' willingness to make that visit.

But Ananias wouldn't have known all that as he slowly made his way down Straight Street. No doubt his feet dragged as he got near the door. No doubt his hand trembled as he knocked. But he obeyed. His approach was simple, friendly and direct. He addressed this murderer as 'Brother Saul', in what was an amazing act of faith. He laid his hands on him in a gesture of friendship. His message was clear and relevant to Saul's situation. He spoke of the Lord Jesus who had sent him. This Jesus could open blind eyes and fill an empty life. And, as we know, Ananias' obedience was rewarded. His visit led to the incorporation of the most notable convert of all time into the Church.

Now, as every parish visitor knows, Sauls are not won on every visit. We have to knock on many doors before we find the response we are hoping for. People these days are suspicious of unknown visitors. They regard their home as their castle. They are not there much, and when they are they don't want to be disturbed. Their favourite TV programme is sure to be on when the visitor calls—and the Church does not enjoy much popularity. 'Anyhow,' you may be thinking, 'I have so much on in my own life. I don't think I want to invest time in what is, frankly, such an unprofitable undertaking.'

Yes, it's easy to think like that. I do it too! But I know it is wrong. I know that there are the occasional Sauls out there who will never darken the door of a church but to whom a wise visitor might minister both healing and conversion, as Ananias did on this occasion. I have been the agent of both in my visits to homes, occasionally. And believe me, I did not want to go. But when we give in to God, as Ananias did, and obey him on this matter, we shall find occasions when it is profoundly fruitful.

We shall find people in need. Lonely people, whom someone from the church could befriend. People with children who have nothing to do, and who could be linked up with one of the organizations in the church. People with talent like music or art, who could be drawn through the use of that gift into the church's life. We shall find some people who seem very antagonistic to start with, but who soon soften as they find that we are not out to bludgeon them or take money from them. We should not be afraid of the apparently tough and intractable like Saul of Tarsus. Think of the change that had taken place in him by the time of that visit! God goes before us in this business. So let's be brave enough to follow him.

An active church can use this approach of visiting in a number of ways.

The vicar can visit. These days many vicars do not—but suppose this one does! He ought particularly to visit those who are just arriving to live in the parish. They will be impressed that the church's leader has taken the trouble to come and see them when they have only just moved in: they will feel that they matter. They will think that this church must be welcoming, and that it might be worth giving it a try, even if they have not been in the habit of going to church. Visiting is important, too, for the vicar himself. He keeps in tune both with people who do not go to church, and with members of the congregation who would love to see more of him than there is time for in church or at meetings.

But it is a great mistake to depend on the minister for visiting; clergy have only a limited amount of time. This is supremely a task that can be shared by many members in the church. It is good to have a team of people who visit regularly. I was visited the other day (as a new resident) by one of the local team—bringing a welcome, a small gift, and a warm feeling left behind. If I had not already begun to worship in that church I think I would have done so.

In some churches there is a special visiting evening so that the team can pray together before they go out, and then come back afterwards to share what has been happening. That can be a great encouragement.

Another form of visitation centres on a particular purpose. It may be that the church is having a special celebration, or a service to which visitors are invited. In such circumstances it is helpful to have some attractive written material about the church and the event in question to leave behind. And the more imaginative and attractively produced this is, the less likely it is to be put in the waste paper bin as soon as the visitor has left.

Sometimes it is very effective to visit a locality and ask people, 'What do you feel is the biggest need in this area?' followed by a second question: 'Is there any particular need in this home that you would allow me to pray with you for?' If they say 'yes', go ahead and pray for them there and then. It is amazing how many people respond positively to such an approach.

I think of several occasions when there has been a Mission in the area and an attractively produced Christian book has been given to every house. If that is offered by a friendly visitor it stands a lot more chance of being read than if it is just pushed through the letter box. And people do find their way to Christian faith through reading books like that, left by a pleasant visitor.

I do not like the idea of visiting to ask for money for the church and its collapsing spire! That gives a completely wrong message to the unchurched. It suggests that Christianity is out to *get* something from them. Instead, as we know, it is all about the generous God who longs to *give* to us. But such visiting is very acceptable for humanitarian causes that Christians and non-Christians alike are concerned about, such as famine relief.

The best visiting is the natural, relaxed, forging of relationships with the people in the same area as ourselves. It does not need to be explicitly 'Christian' at all. But as we get to know them, and they know where we stand, the Christian side will inevitably be noticed, and many people have come to faith in precisely that way. They have become friends with a neighbour. They have noticed and admired that neighbour's friendliness and lifestyle. They have realized that it is something to do with Jesus and church. And they have begun to want to find out for themselves. They might, after all, be missing something!

Occasionally as you visit you will find someone who is just ready to talk. Maybe you have walked in at a time of despair in their lives. Maybe you have come alongside at a time of crisis for some member of the family. Just recently two of my friends were out visiting, and praying for the healing of a team member. On emerging they were angrily accosted by an indignant old lady of 84. Unwittingly, they had parked in front of her house. They were apologetic. They got invited in. They had the privilege of leading that woman to Christ then and there. And they found, subsequently, that her husband was a Christian and had been praying for her conversion for many years!

We simply cannot neglect all the people who do not come to church—not if Jesus has become precious to us. We must do something about it. And visiting is a way we can all attempt. Who knows, we might find we have a great gift for it!

Group material, meditation and prayers

A prayer for the Decade of Evangelism from the Diocese of Hawaii, Episcopal Church of the USA:

Holy Spirit, we pray that in this Decade of Evangelism You will empower your Church more and more with Your many gifts. Give us grateful hearts and a ready tongue to tell our stories and tell forth the Greatest Story on Earth. Lord, help us to renew Your Church in ever new and exciting ways, so that when our Lord

Jesus Christ comes again, He may find a Bride prepared—
prepared for Him who lives and reigns with the Father and the
Holy Spirit, One God, now and forever. Amen.

Follow the prayer with the usual silence and then turn to Acts and ask
three people to read out the passage in parts: a narrator, the Lord, and
Ananias (Paul has nothing to say in this act). Then discuss the
following questions. Again, it would be useful for someone to take
notes of ideas that come up for use in your local church, so that you can
start to make plans.

1. The immense growth of the Jehovah's Witnesses is based on
visiting. And yet they put large numbers of people off. What can we
learn from their zeal, their approach, and their mistakes?

2. How is visiting organized in your church?

3. Can you name three neighbours on each side of your house?
Have you ever been to see them, or had them in? Have you built
relationships with them?

4. Does visiting for a specific purpose happen in your parish? How
is it received?

5. Do you know of people who have been helped, and perhaps
brought into the church, through being visited?

6. Is a note made of new people who visit the church, and a visit
made in the ensuing week?

Meditation

Be still. Take some deep breaths, and as you breathe in, pray. Ask God
to fill you afresh with himself—with his Spirit. As you breathe out, give
to him all your plans, all your hopes, all your troubles. (Let there be a
silence here for a couple of minutes). Now I shall read out that passage
about Ananias and Saul again. Will you imagine that you are Ananias?
Listen to the words. Listen to your own feelings, and get in touch with

your own thoughts. (Read out the passage slowly, and have a moment or two of quiet after you have finished.)

Then ask everyone to say briefly what they felt or thought. After that, have a short time of open prayer.

Final prayers

Some words of Teresa of Avila:

> *Christ has no body now on earth but yours;*
> *yours are the only hands with which he can do his work,*
> *yours are the only feet with which he can go about the world,*
> *yours are the only eyes through which his compassion*
> *can shine forth upon a troubled world.*
> *Christ has no body now on earth but yours.*

From *The Lion Book of Famous Prayers*, compiled by Veronica Zundel

> *Almighty God,*
> *who caused the light of the gospel*
> *to shine throughout the world*
> *through the preaching of your servant Saint Paul:*
> *grant that we who celebrate his wonderful conversion*
> *may follow him in bearing witness to your truth;*
> *through Jesus Christ our Lord.*

Collect for the Conversion of St Paul, *Alternative Service Book*

A prayer for the Decade of Evangelism from the Church of Melanesia:

> *Almighty God, give us your Holy Spirit so that we may have power*
> *to speak about you and not be afraid to spread your Word*
> *throughout the world. May we ourselves show the world your*
> *Word through our actions and know that You are always with us.*
> *Through Jesus Christ our Lord. Amen.*

10 Sharing the Faith Through Your Home

AH! GOOD! HERE'S GEORGE WITH THE COFFEE!

ARE YOU SAVED?

Most of us have homes. And the home is a wonderful asset. Not just for ourselves and our families, but for hospitality and for reaching out to people who are not churchgoers. But it is an asset which we are on the whole slow to use. We should call to mind that most of the spread of the gospel in the early Church was through home meetings. And most of the spread of the gospel in Eastern Europe in the past fifty years (when communism reigned supreme and churches were closed down) was in precisely the same way. Acts chapter 10 gives us a delightful insight into how homes can be used for the spread of the gospel.

At Caesarea there was a man named Cornelius, a centurion in what was known as the Italian Regiment. He and his family were devout and God-fearing; he gave generously to those in need and prayed to God regularly. One day at about three in the afternoon he had a vision. He distinctly saw an angel of God, who came to him and said, 'Cornelius!' Cornelius stared at him in fear. 'What is it, Lord?' he asked. The angel answered, 'Your prayers and gifts to the poor have come up as a memorial offering before God. Now send men to Joppa to bring back a man named Simon who is called Peter. He is staying with Simon the tanner, whose house is by the sea.' When the angel who spoke to him had gone, Cornelius called two of his servants and a devout soldier who was one of his attendants. He told them everything that had happened, and sent them to Joppa. About noon the following day as they were on their journey and approaching the city, Peter went up on the roof to pray. He became hungry, and wanted something to eat, and while the meal was being prepared he fell into a trance.

The story of his vision is well known. It was a divine warning not to call anyone common or unclean. And his obedience was immediately put to the test. Would he go with the emissaries from Cornelius to a Gentile home, or refuse?

While Peter was wondering about the meaning of the vision, the men sent by Cornelius found out where Simon's house was and stopped at the gate. They called out, asking if Simon who was known as Peter was staying there. While Peter was still thinking about the vision, the Spirit said to him, 'Simon, three men are looking for you. So get up and go downstairs. Do not hesitate to go with them, for I have sent them.' Peter went down and said to the men, 'I'm the one you're looking for. Why have you come?' The men replied, 'We have come from Cornelius the centurion. He is a righteous and God-fearing man, who is respected by all the Jewish people. A holy angel told him to have you come to his house so that he could hear what you have to say.' Then Peter invited the men into the house to be his guests. The next day he started out with them, and . . . arrived in Caesarea. Cornelius was expecting them, and had called together his relatives and close friends. As Peter entered the house, Cornelius met him and fell at his feet in reverence. But Peter made him get up. 'Stand up,' he said, 'I am only a man myself.' Talking with him, Peter went inside and found a large gathering of people.

Acts 10:1–10, 17–26

It was an impromptu home meeting, and we recall how Peter took the opportunity of explaining the good news to them, and had the joy of seeing them respond to the gospel and receive a very evident baptism into the realm of the Holy Spirit.

There you have two excellent examples of how the home was used by the early church.

Notice the hospitality offered by Simon the tanner, an otherwise unknown Christian. But he made his home available to his namesake, Simon Peter. And while Peter was having his vision on the flat roof of the little house, a good meal was being prepared downstairs. What is more, when three visitors from a Gentile nation pitched up at the door, Simon the tanner did the unthinkable in those days, and welcomed them in. That meant three more for dinner! It meant social ostracism from the neighbours, in all probability. And it meant an almighty squash in the guest room (if he had one) for the night. Hospitality. That is the name of the game. And it is a very attractive Christian quality, and one which God delights to use in the spread of the gospel.

It is when people see us relaxed in our homes that they feel free to be real with us. The welcome and the food and the care make them feel loved. And it is sometimes the case that we can help even an overnight visitor to faith in Jesus in those circumstances. The Acts record tells us that the Holy Spirit made it plain to Peter that he had sent those three men. Sometimes the Spirit gives us that same conviction about one or more visitors, and the way opens up to talk about Christ.

A friend of mine who knew President Carter well once told me a remarkable story. The President confided in him that he wished he had done many things differently during his term of office. But one thing he would not change. Whenever he had a personal guest in the White House throughout those years, he would find some opportunity of speaking to him or her about Jesus Christ. The visitors might be very ordinary people, or heads of state. It made no difference. The Carters wanted to share the most important aspect of their lives with all who came to their home. That's what hospitality can do for visitors—even when you are as busy as the President of the United States.

Hospitality is one way in which Christians can use their home. But there is another, equally important. The home offers an excellent place for having meetings—and that was the main way in which the gospel spread. Large public meetings did not play a major part in the spread of

Christianity, because they seemed very suspect to a politically sensitive government, always on the lookout for sedition. The account we have just read shows how Cornelius used his home for an evangelistic meeting, even though neither the host nor the guests knew what was going to happen! The home still remains a marvellous setting for small meetings, and is, in fact, the most natural place in the world in which to discuss the Christian faith.

I look back at some of the ways I have used my home for this purpose. I think of early days in a curacy and the mad evenings of games we used to have for students at a nearby College of Education. Afterwards I would give a talk on the way to a personal faith. I think of several for whom Jesus become real through those meetings—one of them now a missionary in Afghanistan.

I think of the way a doctor, a hotelier, a dentist and I pooled the names of friends and contacts, whom we then invited to a meeting in a large home. We did this five times a year, and a very high proportion of those invited came, for the simple reason that they were our friends. We made sure to have a well-known and interesting layman come to speak, and one by one many of these friends of ours became committed Christians. And the whole thing was so relaxed: everybody loved it, whether they became Christians or not.

No less relaxed was the night when the whole of a university hockey team came to stay in our house, because one of our children was in the team. The fun and laughter which marked that evening made it very easy the next morning to leave some copies of evangelistic books of mine on the breakfast table for anyone to take if they were interested. They all went.

I think of other occasions when we have simply had one or two other couples in for supper and in the course of the meal it has seemed natural to raise the question of Jesus. If they have wanted to pursue the conversation, we have been delighted to do so, and have seen many people come to Christ as a result. If they were not ready to talk about it naturally we moved on to another topic of conversation. It is important, like Peter in the account we have just read, to be listening to the Holy Spirit; not to try to batter down doors that are not open but to sense which doors the Lord has unlocked before us, and is just waiting for us to nudge open.

Sometimes it is not just a couple, but a houseful. I recall going to speak at one such event and I found it packed to the doors and up the stairs. Even the bedrooms were wired up to the microphone which had been set up downstairs! A crush like that has its own impact even before anyone begins to speak. It was a very profitable evening.

A home is so versatile. I think of meetings for enquirers into the Christian faith which we often had in our home, usually preceded by a meal. Many committed Christians have wives, husbands or relatives who do not share their faith and will not come to church. It will be pointless to press them: they simply aren't at home in a church setting. But many of them would gladly come to a meeting in a home (with a meal!) where they would be with other enquirers and know they can have a no-holds-barred series of encounters with an informed Christian. They love the challenge of it and think they are in no danger. But they are! Both from the impact of truth and from the prayers of their loved ones in the background, I have known many people come to faith through such groups.

Something rather similar is the home group for new believers. If your church is one where there is, from time to time, a clear evangelistic challenge then you will need small nurture groups to help those who respond. These are best run in homes. Invariably, you will find that some have come and enlisted in one of these nurture groups without ever having taken the step of surrender to Christ. And so, while there is nurture for all in the close fellowship which soon develops in such a group, there is also, for some, an evangelistic dimension as well.

There are all sorts of other ways of using the home. It is an ideal place for an investigative Bible study, for instance. Or for viewing a video of some film which makes it easy to speak about the Lord: films like *Chariots of Fire*, *Babette's Feast*, *The Mission* spring to mind as being effective discussion starters a few years ago. Always one or two new films like these come out each year.

In a way, *how* we use our house (if we have one) is not important. What matters is that we *do* use it. It is a great privilege and a great joy. I have an old settee which I see as holy ground. For over the years many people have knelt at it and surrendered their lives to Christ. Praise God for the home!

Group material, meditation and prayers

A prayer for the Decade of Evangelism from the Church in Australia:

Grant us, Lord God
the vision of your Kingdom,
forgiveness and new life,
and the stirring of your Spirit;
so that we may
share your vision,
proclaim your love,
and change this world,
in the Name of Christ. Amen.

Slowly read out the passage from Acts at the start of this chapter—and before you begin, ask people to shut their eyes and listen to the words, and visualize the scene. Then discuss the following questions.

1. Discuss from the experience of the group what use each person has made of the home for evangelism.

2. Think of ways in which you could use your home for some event in church life designed for non-members who might find the church building itself a deterrent.

3. Think of ways you could use your home evangelistically for young people or colleagues at work or relations.

4. Discuss ways of opening up conversation about the gospel at a small supper party in your home.

Meditation

Be still. Now be aware of the presence and the promise of Jesus: 'Where two or three are gathered together in my name, there am I in the midst of them.' Then in your mind's eye see the place where you live. Still be aware of the presence of Jesus with you, there. Lord Jesus Christ, you went into people's homes when you lived here as a man. Just a few people's homes then. But now it can be many people's. In many countries—many places. Lord Jesus Christ, please come into my home. And now, please give us wisdom, each one of us, and ideas, on how to use our home for you. (Have three or four minutes' silence, then pray.) Lord Jesus Christ, come afresh into our hearts and into our homes. Let us know your presence and your power. Amen.

Spend a short time going round the group and asking each person for any idea that has come to them. Follow that with a time of open prayer.

Final prayer

Lord, I've discovered it's never a secret
When you live in a home
For you simply cannot be hid.
The neighbours soon know you are there
Even strangers learn of your presence.
When you are the Great First in a home
There is a radiance that speaks of joy
There is gentleness, kindness,
Laughter and love.
There is commotion mixed with contentment
There are problems mixed with prayer.
Lord, your own Word says it so vividly:
'It was known that he was in the house.'

Ruth Harms Calkin, from *Lord I Keep Running Back To You*, copyright © Tyndale House Publishers Inc., 1979. Taken from *The Lion Prayer Collection*

11 Sharing the Faith Through Personal Conversation

Time and again I have been in Christian meetings when, as a matter of interest, we have been asked what was the most significant factor in bringing us to faith. And time and again it was not a famous preacher, not a big meeting, not a church service. No, it was one friend, a Christian, who really cared, and was not afraid to talk about Jesus.

Not surprisingly we find this happening in the Acts. The most famous example comes where Philip meets the Ethiopian eunuch. We glanced at it in Chapter 3 but we have much to gain from looking at the passage in more detail.

Now the angel of the Lord said to Philip, 'Go south to the road—the desert road—which goes down from Jerusalem to Gaza.' So he started out, and on his way he met an Ethiopian eunuch, an important official in charge of all the treasury of Candace, queen of the Ethiopians. This man had gone to Jerusalem to worship, and on his way home was sitting in his chariot reading the book of Isaiah the prophet. The Spirit told Philip, 'Go to that chariot and stay near it.' Then Philip ran up to the chariot and heard the man reading Isaiah the prophet. 'Do you understand what you are reading?' Philip asked. 'How can I,' he said, 'unless someone explains it to me?' So he invited Philip to come up and sit with him. The eunuch was reading this passage of Scripture: 'He was led as a sheep to the slaughter, and as a lamb before the shearer is silent, so he did not open his mouth. In his humiliation he was deprived of justice. Who can speak of his descendants? For his life was taken from the earth.'

The eunuch asked Philip, 'Tell me, please, who is the prophet talking about, himself or someone else?' Then Philip began with that very passage of Scripture and told him the good news about Jesus. As they travelled along the road they came to some water and the eunuch said, 'Look, here is water. Why shouldn't I be baptised?' And he gave orders to stop the chariot. Then both Philip and the eunuch went down into the water and Philip baptised him. When they came up out of the water the Spirit of the Lord suddenly took Philip away and the eunuch did not see him again, but went on his way rejoicing.

Acts 8:26–39

There are lots of ways of using personal conversation to help someone to find Christ. The simplest of all we mentioned at the end of Chapter 8. It is issuing an invitation to somewhere where the good news will be clearly proclaimed. It is saying, like those disciples in the first chapter of John's Gospel, 'Come and see.' That is how Simon Peter found Jesus. That is how Nathanael found Jesus. Just three words, issued as a warm and honest invitation. It can be very effective.

Another way is to tell someone, quite simply, the difference Christ has begun to make in your own life. The woman of Samaria (John chapter 4) is a classic example of this. After that life-transforming interview with Jesus, she ran back to the men she knew so well and said, 'Come, see a man who told me everything I ever did. Could this be the Christ?' Not much, but quite enough to get them interested! And before long they had discovered Jesus for themselves.

Or think of the blind man whom Jesus healed (John 9:25). He gave him a wonderful testimonial, when the intellectual Pharisees tried to confuse him with theological arguments, maintaining that Jesus must be a sinner if he had healed the man on the Sabbath day. 'Whether he is a sinner or not, I don't know,' was the robust reply. 'One thing I do know. I was blind, but now I see!' That proved unanswerable. Simple, direct testimony to what Jesus has done for us *is* unanswerable, and is a powerful lever in helping people to faith.

But what we find Philip doing with the Ethiopian is something more. He is using conversation to help an enquirer discover the Saviour. Now we shall never find a situation which is even remotely parallel to this African financier reading aloud in his chariot as he sped through the desert. But we can learn from Philip some helpful hints on how we, in our generation, may be able to chat to enquirers about our Lord to such good effect that they find him personally.

Perhaps the first thing that strikes us about Philip in this incident is this. Here is a man who **lives close to God**. He is in touch. The Lord can say to him, 'Go south' and he goes without argument. The Lord can say to him, 'Join this chariot' and he does. I don't imagine it was any audible voice; just an inner hunch. He responded to it—and he could see, with hindsight, that it was indeed the will of God. We need to be a bit more sensitive to those hunches we get from time to time. They may well be from the Lord. If they are not and we make a mistake, nothing is lost. If we are right, we may find ourselves being as helpful to somebody else as Philip was.

I am no less struck by his **humility**. Philip was a very gifted man. There was a religious revival going on in the unlikely place of Samaria—and he was the preacher. He could easily have said 'No' to that hunch that he should go south. 'What's the point of going there? Nobody lives in that desert tract. Anyhow, I'm needed at the meeting tonight.' But he did not say that. He went. God cannot use us if we are proud. He will gladly use the humble, irrespective of their talents and gifts. If we humbly put ourselves at his disposal we shall find him giving us more opportunities than we know how to make use of.

Another thing Philip teaches me is how important it is to **listen**. It is no good rushing in with all sorts of good advice if we have not listened carefully to the other person. Often they will tell you, 'My, how you've helped me,' when in fact you have not said a word. What has happened is that they have poured out their heart to you—and that in itself is therapeutic. We need to become good and discriminating listeners.

Sensitivity is another quality which Philip displayed. He did not barge in with some prearranged sermon; he asked if he could be of any help. No wonder the Ethiopian asked him to come and sit with him; and it was not until Philip saw that the man really wanted to know that he took him further in explaining about Jesus. We need to be relaxed and natural, ready to move on or off spiritual things without batting an eyelid. Such naturalness and sensitivity will prove invaluable, and some of us may need to learn how to be relaxed in this way, through prayer and through practice.

I like his **enthusiasm**, too. Here was Philip in the desert. I have been in that desert. The temperature often soars into the 40s°C. And he ran, yes *ran*, in that heat, so that he should not miss this opportune moment when it came. I know it is fashionable to be 'cool' these days, but people still respond to genuine enthusiasm. Watch the reaction to someone announcing their engagement, or that they have just won a million on the pools. Enthusiasm is infectious all right. If we are thrilled with Jesus, that will be infectious. If we are not, that will be infectious too.

What is more, Philip **knew his stuff**. Now of course, you don't normally find commuters reading Isaiah 53, but it is nice to be able to recognize it when you do! Scripture has a very powerful impact, which presumably is why Philip began with that passage of Scripture and let it speak with all its innate authority. It was not difficult to lead the man to Jesus from there. But it did require some insight and skill. We need to learn the art of beginning wherever the other person happens to be and then (preferably using some appropriate Scripture if we know one) moving on from there to speak directly about Jesus.

And that, of course, is precisely what Philip does. The centre of his message is **Jesus**. And Isaiah is only important as a springboard for launching the discussion onto Jesus. Philip showed the Ethiopian how that passage was wonderfully fulfilled in Jesus. He showed him that Jesus had 'borne our iniquities', and how 'after the suffering of his soul, he had seen the light of life'.

This must have led, naturally and inevitably, to his asking the Ethiopian how he would **respond** to love like that. The response was immediate and full-blooded. 'Look, here is water. Why shouldn't I be baptised?' And he was. Baptism often followed immediately on profession of faith in those days, and perhaps it still should.

Here, then, are some important hints on how to talk to a serious enquirer. If we keep in close touch with God he will give us opportunities. If we walk humbly with our God we won't put people off. If we learn to listen to people, and are sensitive (scratching them where they itch, so to speak), we shall be very acceptable to our not-yet-Christian friends. Better still if we know a bit of the Scriptures and can take people to some of the foundation truths of the faith, so that they can read and assess them for themselves. Our enthusiasm will speak for itself, and if we keep the spotlight firmly on Jesus and the need to respond to him, we shall, in all probability, have the great joy of seeing some of our friends come to the point of saying, 'Look, I think I believe now. Why shouldn't I be baptized?'

Group material and prayers

A prayer for the Decade of Evangelism from the Church of the West Indies:

> *Almighty God, our heavenly Father, the privilege is ours to be*
> *called to share in the loving, healing and reconciling mission of*
> *your Son Jesus Christ our Lord in this age and wherever we are.*
> *Since without you we can do no good thing:*
> *may your Spirit make us wise;*
> *may your Spirit guide us;*
> *may your Spirit renew us;*
> *may your Spirit strengthen us*
> *so that we will be:*
> *strong in faith;*
> *discerning in proclamation;*
> *courageous in witness;*
> *persistent in good deeds.*
> *This we ask through the same Jesus Christ our Lord. Amen.*

Make sure that every member of the group has the passage from Acts chapter 8 in front of them. Read the passage out slowly, and ask people to follow the words and to imagine they are hearing them for the first time.

Then spend five minutes in silence while everyone looks at the passage.

Ask people to shut their eyes for a couple of minutes and to think and pray about what they have read.

Then ask them to open their eyes. Go round the group, and ask each person to say very briefly what thought came to them. They can say, 'I pass' if they want to! Then discuss the following questions.

1 Why are we so shy of speaking in a direct way about Jesus?

2. Do you know two or three verses of Scripture which would be helpful in guiding an honest enquirer to the Saviour?

3. How would you end a conversation such as this, if your friend wanted to take the step of commitment?

4. Which of these three approaches (invitation, testimonial or conversation) do you find most congenial—and why?

Final prayers

God our Father, we pray for those who have never appreciated the riches which you offer them in your Son Jesus; those for whom he has never become a reality;
for those who have never been moved by the story of the cross or felt the need of the forgiveness Jesus won for us;
for those who leave the gospel aside as something that does not concern them; which they feel they can get on well enough without; for those for whom 'Christ' is only a swear-word.
For all these, and for all who do not pray for themselves, accept our intercessions, through Jesus Christ our Lord.

Reproduced from *Further Everyday Prayers* edited by Hazel Snashall with the permission of the National Christian Education Council. Taken from *The Lion Prayer Collection*

Eternal God and Father,
you create us by your power;
and redeem us by your love;
guide and strengthen us by your Spirit,
that we may give ourselves in love and service
to one another and to you;
through Jesus Christ our Lord.

Alternative Service Book

Invite people to pray their own prayers, if they wish to.

Then have a time of silence, and tell people that it will last for three or four minutes and that you will end it with a prayer.

A prayer for the Decade of Evangelism from the Church of Tanzania:

O God, Giver of life and source of all wisdom, grant us Your power and might; shine in us Your bright Light; penetrate our hearts; and clean out all our doubts and emptiness.

Enable us in this Decade of Evangelism
to reach the unreached,
to support the underprivileged
to shine as Your Light in the darkness
and to encourage one another.

Make each of us feel concern and challenge; send us out in Your power to do your will. We ask this in the Name of Your Son, Our Saviour, Jesus Christ the Lord. Amen.

12   Sharing the Faith Through Teams

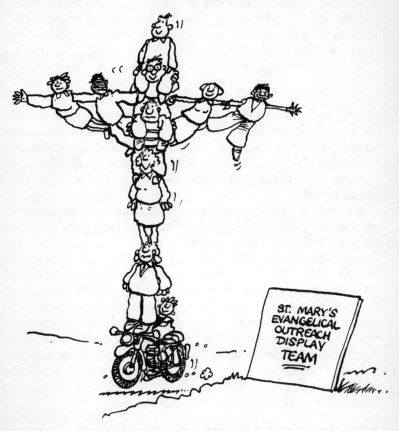

ST. MARY'S
EVANGELICAL
OUTREACH
DISPLAY
TEAM

One of the easiest, most delightful and most fruitful ways of sharing the faith is for a team of people to do it together. They were well aware of this in the days of the Acts. Not only do we always hear the disciples referred to as 'the Twelve', but we find Peter and John, Stephen and his six colleagues, Paul and Barnabas, Barnabas and Mark, Paul, Silas and Timothy and the rest working in teams. Here is a typical example:

> While they were worshipping the Lord and fasting, the Holy Spirit said, 'Set apart for me Barnabas and Saul for the work to which I have called them.' So after they had fasted and prayed, they placed their hands on them and sent them off. The two of them, sent on their way by the Holy Spirit, went down to Seleucia and sailed from there to Cyprus. When they arrived at Salamis, they proclaimed the word of God in the Jewish synagogues. John was with them as their helper.
>
> Acts 13:2–5

The idea of the team was not new. Many rabbis went round in groups teaching and preaching. Jesus himself had made a point of associating his disciples with himself in all the ministry he did. And on the day of Pentecost we find Peter being the spokesman but the 'team' of the rest of the apostles being there with him, involved in the worship, praise and testimony.

It is obviously a good idea. One in the partnership can encourage and support the other. One can pray while another speaks. One can supplement the shortcomings of another.

Sometimes these apostolic teams did not work out too happily. The first one didn't. We read that quite soon John Mark left Paul and Barnabas for some undisclosed reason, and returned to Jerusalem (13:13). Paul was not prepared to trust him again, though Barnabas, Mark's cousin, was. Indeed their disagreement over this led to different spheres of ministry for Paul and Barnabas. We never hear of their working together again, though it is lovely to see that towards the end of his life, Paul can write: 'Get Mark and bring him with you, because he is helpful to me in my ministry' (2 Timothy 4:11). Here is Luke's account of the incident.

> Some time later Paul said to Barnabas, 'Let us go back and visit the brothers in all the towns where we preached the word of the Lord, and see how they are doing.' Barnabas wanted to take John, also called Mark, with them. But Paul did not think it wise to take him, because he had deserted them in Pamphylia and had not

continued with them in the work. They had such a sharp disagreement that they parted company. Barnabas took Mark and sailed for Cyprus, but Paul chose Silas and left, commended by the brothers to the grace of the Lord. He went through Syria and Cilicia, strengthening the churches. He came to Derbe and then to Lystra, where a disciple named Timothy lived... The brothers at Lystra and Iconium spoke well of him. Paul wanted to take him along on the journey.

Acts 15:36—16:3

It is sad when Christians disagree. Sad, too when it happens in a team, so that others share in the divisiveness. But God can overrule our failures, and he did in this case, by using two teams instead of one, and by reinstating John Mark both in the ministry and in the affections of Paul. But the interesting thing is that, despite the division, they did not resort to the 'one man band' (which characterizes the ministry in so many churches). They knew teams to be so important that both leaders got a team around them before they went off on renewed mission.

Why are teams so valuable? There are a number of reasons. They deliver us from the tyranny and the failings of one-person leadership. They enable different gifts to find a place and flourish. They offer graduated opportunity for ministry. Some may not say a word, but simply drive the car. Some may sing or play or act. Some may give testimony, in a short interview, to the difference Christ has made to them. Everyone is stretched and enriched by the experience. They learn a lot by planning the enterprise with care beforehand. They learn a lot by joining together in doing it, out of love for Christ and for the people they go to serve. And as they debrief afterwards, and consider the strengths and weaknesses of what took place, they are equipping themselves for further ministry in the future.

If, instead of a visiting preacher being sent to one church from another, a small team takes on the project, important lessons get learnt.

◆ The church being visited will appreciate the value of every-member ministry far more by experiencing the presence of a team than from many addresses on the subject given by just one person, however eloquent.

105

◆ They will not just *hear* the message of God's reconciling grace in the preaching. They will actually *see* it in the team's mutual relationships. And what we see in action goes much deeper than what we are told.

◆ They will see that we don't have to be professionals to engage in ministry for God. Ordinary people with an extraordinary Lord can have a great impact for him.

◆ They will see that every member of the team has a place.

◆ They will recognize the prayer and preparation that have gone on in the background.

◆ They will sense the vibrancy of a church where ministry clearly does not reside in the vicar alone but in the whole body, of whom the team are a small sample.

What if it all goes wrong, and disastrous mistakes happen? It does not matter a bit. Those on the receiving end say to themselves, 'A good idea, that was. But it didn't quite go to plan. I reckon we could put on as good a show as that.' And before you know where you are, the infection of the team idea has spread to the receiving church and they are looking for an opportunity to go out and try it!

In any case, the enthusiasm generated by the event will need a channel of expression, and it is good for one or two of the team to be interviewed in the next week's notices of the sending church. This not only gives the news, but it imparts the thrill of ministering together, and it will be surprising if the leader of the team does not get asked by an aggrieved Mr Jones or Mrs Green why he did not take them on his team! To which the answer is, 'Great, you shall come next time.'

Another great advantage of the team is that it is so flexible: it can be used in many ways. The church where I have just come to live has a visiting team, a leadership team, a healing team, a music team, a youth leaders' team, and a drama team. I guess there are others that I have not discovered in my two weeks here! But it does mean that the congregation is buzzing with life and with commitment. People have a stake in the enterprise. The church is not just somewhere where they worship on Sundays.

During my ministry I have worked with teams of many sorts.

First and foremost, a staff team: vicar, curate(s), secretary, caretaker, youth worker—they are all part of the staff team, if you happen to work in a multiple-staff church. Their relationships, their job fulfilment, their opportunity to share encouragements and disappointments with their peers, is very important, because hurts can arise so easily, and then there is tension at the heart of the team.

I have also found that it is vital to have a lay leadership team. These will include the wardens and music director, and chair or vice-chair of the PCC, but will also have on the team gifted, mature Christians who have a particular ministry in the church: maybe they head up a home group or the visitation ministry.

Then there is the music. To turn a choir into a music team is a delicate but necessary art. It has nothing to do with whether one sings new songs or old: it has everything to with the love and laughter and sharing which goes on. As the people in that group begin to share their lives together, so the music begins to flow. In a church where I used to serve the music ministry became celebrated: not because of the inherent quality of the voices, but because two-thirds of every Friday evening was taken up with a meal, news, needs, and praying together. It was because of this quality of relationship that the music became something beautiful for God.

On that same Friday evening a group who had discovered that they had dramatic gifts also got together—for supper, mutual ministry and creativity. Here again, relationships were the key. And out of that cohesive team came short dramatic sketches that added a great power to the preached word and were good enough to use—as they were used—on nationwide television, and in ministering with Billy Graham.

The point is plain. Shared ministry is an enormous strength. The apostles found that. We read that these teams of theirs were invaluable, both for evangelizing on their missions, and for strengthening the disciples—as some were helped by one member of the team, some by another.

How, you may ask, can such teams be used in evangelism? Very simply.

It may be that your church is asked to provide a speaker for a **single event**. Why not suggest that a team, not simply an individual, shall come? I have found that this is almost always accepted (even though the inviters may be mystified!). But they won't be mystified for long when the team use their different gifts in leading the worship with freshness and reverence, illustrating the theme with dramatic sketches and perhaps enriching the worship with liturgical dance.

Simple, down-to-earth testimony is an added ingredient that is often not used in church. And more than one person can take the talk. Add to that the opportunity for personal prayer with members of the team after the event is over, and people will go away with a new joy in their hearts and a new understanding of Christian ministry.

Or perhaps your church is invited to lead a **weekend** in another congregation. Here again a team is worth its weight in gold. I have found that a good pattern for such an event is to take a leading lay member of the team in with me to a special meeting of the PCC on the Friday night to talk over with them principles of spiritual renewal and lay involvement in a congregation—while other members of the team speak at a few supper parties where members of the receiving congregation have invited their unchurched friends.

Sometimes they will have the joy of helping a guest at such a supper party to personal faith. Always they will point forward to the Sunday morning service, which will be evangelistic, and encourage everyone present to come.

Saturday sees a half-day Parish Conference. It begins with reverent but lively worship and teaching, followed by coffee. Then people split up into various seminar groups (the subjects have been chosen by the receiving parish beforehand; and this has, of course, affected the make-up of the visiting team).

The conference could end with a lovely informal Eucharist and time for personal ministry. The evening might see the team taking a special youth meeting.

And, in addition to the evangelistic service to which church members would bring their friends on the Sunday morning (again, carefully prepared, with nurture groups in place for the follow-up), there could be a final celebratory Eucharist on the Sunday night before the team drives back, exhausted but exhilarated, to their home parish. Such visits are a great tonic all round.

The whole thing can be enlarged if a **parish mission** is held. Here longer planning and a much larger team are needed, but the principles of every-member ministry, of unity and prayer, of faith and risk, and of using God-given gifts are just the same. There is something very special in going off with a team from the parish for a week to bear the torch of witness aloft for Christ in another place. If you are interested in pursuing the subject, why not get hold of my book *Evangelism through the Local Church* (Hodder and Stoughton), which shows how such outreaches can be planned and carried out?

I'm glad to have taken this subject of faith-sharing through teams as our final study because it exhibits so clearly what the church is for. It is not a stage for gifted individuals to strut on. It is a family of brothers and sisters: men, women and children from a tremendous variety of backgrounds, adopted by God into his family, and put to work together in the family business. That business involves bearing unashamed witness to Jesus, the one who can make new men and women of us. And it involves doing it in partnership with one another in the family, under the sovereign hand of the great God whom we serve, without whose power nothing can happen at all.

The wonderful thing is that when we do reach out, in fear and trembling, as members of that family, as part of that team, God does wing our words and use our halting speech. He does allow something of his beauty to be seen in our lives and relationships, despite all that needs to be improved. And he extends through us, his incompetent disciples, the work that Jesus came on earth to do—to bring men and women to God and to the new life he offers them.

What a privilege to be part of such an enterprise!

Group material, meditation and prayers

A prayer for the Decade of Evangelism from the Church in Wales:

> *Lord, open to us the sea of your mercy*
> *and water us with full streams*
> *from the riches of your grace*
> *and the springs of your kindness.*

Make us children of your peace,
kindle in us the fire of your love,
show in us the fear and love of your name,
strengthen our weakness,
and bind us close to you and to each other
as we share in your mission to the world:
to your glory, Father, Son and Holy Spirit. Amen.

Read out the passages from Acts 13:2–5 and 15:36—16:3. Spend a few moments of quiet while people look at the passages (either in the Bible or in the book).

Then discuss the following questions:

1. Can you see advantages—and disadvantages—in the use of the team?

2. How could such teams be set up and trained in your church?

3. Let someone who has been involved in outreach as part of a team relate his or her experiences.

4. In what ways does a team exhibit, and not only proclaim, the good news?

Meditation

Please get yourself comfortable ... with your back straight. Let your feet rest on the floor, and let your hands rest on your knees. Be aware of your own breathing. Be aware of the people around you. The risen Christ is with us now, as he said he would be. Think about Jesus's promise of the Holy Spirit ...

On the last and greatest day of the Feast, Jesus stood and said in a loud voice, 'If anyone is thirsty, let him come to me and drink. Whoever believes in me, as the Scripture has said, streams of living water will flow from within him.' By this he meant the Spirit, whom those who believed in him were later to receive. Up to that time the Spirit had not been given, since Jesus had not yet

110

been glorified. On hearing his words, some of the people said, 'Surely this man is the Prophet.' Others said, 'He is the Christ.'

John 7:37–41

Lord Jesus Christ, we're thirsty . . . so we come to you now, and we drink. Lord Jesus Christ, you're glorified now. Give us your Spirit. May the streams of living water flow out of us—into your dry and thirsty world. Lord Jesus Christ, you were anointed with the Spirit . . . and that word 'anointed' means Christed. The anointed one of God . . . the Christed one. And now you can fill us with that Spirit. So we ask, now, that you will . . . so that we can share the good news—so that people can know your forgiveness, so that people can know your love, and so that people can know you. (Now spend four or five minutes in silence.)

Then ask people to pray their own prayers aloud, if they want to.

Final prayer

Lord God, as we set about this work
we ask that you will lead us step by step.
Help us to see with your eyes.
Help us to listen with your ears.
Help us to think about what we are doing in our world.
Guide us to recognize how great are our resources,
and inspire us to put our plans, your plans, into action.
Lord, for your sake, and for the sake of those around us,
may we not falter nor make empty plans
but work to share your love and grace.

From *Mission Pursuit*, copyright © Council for World Mission
Taken from *The Lion Prayer Collection*